THE ORIGINS OF MEXICAN NATIONAL POLITICS

1808-1847

They All Want to Be President

"$36,000 and what one can . . ."

The ORIGINS OF MEXICAN NATIONAL POLITICS

1808-1847

Edited by Jaime E. Rodríguez O.

SR
BOOKS

A Scholarly Resources Inc. Imprint
Wilmington, Delaware

Scholarly Resources Inc.
104 Greenhill Avenue
Wilmington, DE 19805-1897

Frontispiece: From *El Universal*, 1853

Library of Congress Cataloging-in-Publication Data

The origins of Mexican national politics, 1808–1847 / edited by Jaime E.
    Rodríguez O.
        p.   cm. — (Latin American silhouettes)
    "This volume consists of four essays which appeared in a book . . .
entitled the Evolution of the Mexican political system. That work resulted
from a colloquium held at the University of California, Irvine, on April 28–
29, 1990"—Pref.
    Includes bibliographical references (p.   ) and index.
    Contents: Politicization of the Army of New Spain during the War of
Independence, 1810–1821 / Christon I. Archer — The first popular elections
in Mexico City, 1812–1813 / Virginia Guedea — The Constitution of 1824
and the formation of the Mexican State / Jaime E. Rodríguez O. — The
making of a fait accompli: Mexico and the Provincias Internas, 1776–1846 /
Barbara A. Tenenbaum.
    ISBN 0-8420-2723-8 (pbk. : alk. paper)
    1. Mexico—Politics and government—1810-   —Congresses. 2. Civil-
military relations—Mexico—History—19th century—Congresses.
3. Political participation—Mexico—History—19th century—Congresses.
4. Elections—Mexico—Mexico City—History—19th century—
Congresses. 5. Mexico—Armed Forces—Political activity—History—
19th century. 6. Mexico—Constitutional history—Congresses.
7. Nationalism—Mexico—History—19th century—Congresses.
I. Rodríguez O., Jaime E., 1940-   . II. Evolution of the Mexican
political system. III. Series.
JL1231.074   1997
320.972'09'034—dc21   97-17583
                                                                          CIP

recycled paper

To the scholars of the
Instituto de Investigaciones Históricas
Universidad Nacional Autónoma de México
and especially to the members of its
Seminario de Rebeliones y Revoluciones en México

Contents

Preface

THIS VOLUME consists of four essays that appeared in a book that I edited entitled *The Evolution of the Mexican Political System*. That work resulted from a colloquium held at the University of California, Irvine, on April 28–29, 1990. Its twelve chapters, some written in English and some in Spanish, examined the politics and political processes of Mexico during the nineteenth and twentieth centuries. The volume was well received by reviewers and the public and is now out of print. Comments by a number of generous colleagues, among them Colin M. MacLachlan, William Beezley, and Paul Vanderwood, convinced me that the essays by Christon I. Archer, Virginia Guedea, myself, and Barbara A. Tenenbaum constituted a useful introduction to the politics of early independent Mexico. Therefore, I proposed to Richard Hopper that SR Books reissue those essays under the title *The Origins of Mexican National Politics* so that they might reach a larger public. Fortunately, Mr. Hopper and his colleagues at Scholarly Resources agreed.

Once again, I thank all those who contributed to the publication of the earlier work. In addition, I thank Linda Pote Musumeci, senior editor at Scholarly Resources, for all her help with this new edition.

This volume, like *The Evolution of the Mexican Political System*, is dedicated to the scholars of the Instituto de Investigaciones Históricas at the Universidad Nacional Autónoma de México (UNAM) who kindly have received me and generously have provided me with an intellectual home in their country during the past fifteen years. I am particularly grateful to the members of the Instituto's Seminario de Rebeliones y Revoluciones en México who for years have listened patiently to my ideas and offered incisive but supportive criticism. In addition, I have had the good fortune of benefiting from their ideas and their work.

Jaime E. Rodríguez O.

Los Angeles
April 26, 1997

Contributors

Christon I. Archer is professor of history at the University of Calgary. He has written extensively on the army of New Spain and on the insurgency. His works include *The Army in Bourbon Mexico* (Albuquerque, 1977), which won the Bolton Prize. He is currently working on the insurgency and counterinsurgency during the struggle for independence.

Virginia Guedea is research professor at the Instituto de Investigaciones Históricas of the Universidad Nacional Autónoma de México and associate editor of the journal *Mexican Studies/Estudios Mexicanos* as well as visiting research professor at the Instituto de Investigaciones Dr. José María Luis Mora. She has published many studies of insurrections, the military, secret societies, and the origins of national politics, particularly during the Independence period. Her works include *La insurgencia en el Departamento del Norte: Los Llanos de Apan y la Sierra de Puebla, 1810–1816* (Mexico, 1996).

Jaime E. Rodríguez O. is professor of history at the University of California, Irvine, and editor of the journal *Mexican Studies/Estudios Mexicanos*. He has published widely on the early nineteenth century. His works include *La independencia de la América española* (Mexico, 1996).

Barbara A. Tenenbaum is editor in chief of the *Encyclopedia of Latin American History*. She is also the specialist in Mexican culture at the Library of Congress. She has published widely on nineteenth-century Mexican finances. Her works include *The Politics of Penury: Debts and Taxes in Mexico, 1821–1856* (Albuquerque, 1986). She is currently working on the evolution of Mexico City in the late nineteenth century.

Introduction

Jaime E. Rodríguez O.

> Was it probable, was it possible, that . . . a free government
> . . . should be introduced and established among such a
> people, over that vast continent, or any part of it? It appeared
> to me . . . as absurd as . . . [it] would be to establish
> democracies among the birds, beasts, and fishes.

John Adams[1]

> Does . . . [he] know that the despotism which the English
> exercised over their colonies and the slavery which those
> [lands] endured has never existed in the [Spanish] Americas?

Servando Teresa de Mier[2]

WHILE MOST SCHOLARS TODAY would reject John Adams's blatant
bigotry, it is not clear that they would deny his judgment about the ability
of Mexicans to establish a democracy. In contrast to the congratulatory
nature of most writing on the emergence of the United States, historians
appear diffident, almost embarrassed, about the birth of Mexico. Although
"a monarchical society [was transformed] into a democratic one," no
Mexican Gordon Wood proclaims that it was "unlike any that had ever
existed. . . . [Nor that] it was one of the greatest revolutions the world has

---

[1] John Adams, *The Works of John Adams*, 10 vols. (Boston: Little, Brown,
and Company, 1850–1856), 10:145.

[2] Servando Teresa de Mier, "Memoria político-instructiva enviada desde
Filadelfia en agosto de 1821 a los gefes independientes del Anáhuac, llamado por
los españoles Nueva España," in *La formación de un republicano*, vol. 4 of *Obras
Completas*, ed. Jaime E. Rodríguez O. (Mexico: Universidad Nacional Autónoma
de México, 1988), 164.

known . . ., [or that it] was as radical and social as any revolution in history."[3] Mexican historians do not assume such a smug, triumphant tone in discussing their emancipation. On the contrary, most agree with the distinguished historian Luis Villoro who, following José María Luis Mora, refers to the Mexican Revolution of Independence as "la revolución desdichada," the unfortunate revolution.[4]

The term seemed apt inasmuch as the great insurgent leaders, Miguel Hidalgo and José María Morelos, were defeated and executed by the royalists. And, if we are to believe Villoro, the "people" lost faith in political options.[5] Independence finally came in 1821 when the royalist officer Agustín de Iturbide changed sides and convinced the royal army to support him. Again, as Villoro interprets the process, "the colonial oligarchy had managed to contain the revolution. . . . Once more, the *letrados* [lawyers] of the middle class took the initiative. But now the popular revolution had ended and the *letrados* had lost true contact with the people."[6] His conclusion is particularly significant; in referring to the founders of the First Federal Republic in 1824, he declares, "To establish the government . . ., they no longer relied on the people, but on their alliance with a fraction of the army. [That was] because true power remained in the hands of privileged groups: the Church and the army, above all. Many years of struggle would be necessary to transform the social reality upon which their privileges rested: unfortunate years, which would, ultimately, lead to the desired Reform."[7]

Villoro, like many historians of Mexico, characterizes the early republican years as a lost era, a period of economic decline, political chaos, and military catastrophe that only ended in the 1860s. Indeed, many have defined the transformations of the 1850s and 1860s, the Reform, and the struggle under the leadership of Benito Juárez—first against the conservatives, and later against the French and Maximilian—as the time

---

[3]For Gordon Wood's triumphant claims about the United States see his *The Radicalism of the American Revolution* (New York: Alfred A. Knopf, 1992), 5.

[4]Luis Villoro, *El proceso ideológico de la revolución de la independencia*, 2d ed. (Mexico: UNAM, 1977), 215 and passim. See also his account, "La revolución de independencia," in *Historia general de México*, 4 vols. (Mexico: El Colegio de México, 1976), 2:303–356. There are reasons for the difference in attitudes in the two North American nations; the United States rose to great power in the nineteenth century, while Mexico experienced economic decline, political chaos, and military defeat during that same period. I have discussed some of these questions in my earlier work. See my *Down from Colonialism: Mexico's Nineteenth-Century Crisis* (Los Angeles: Chicano Studies Research Center, 1983); and my "La paradoja de la independencia de México," *Secuencia: Revista de historia y ciencias sociales* 21 (September–December 1991): 7–17.

[5]Villoro, "La revolución de independencia," 2:346.

[6]Ibid., 2:346, 352.

[7]Ibid., 2:356.

when the nation was truly formed.[8] Thus, unlike the United States, the founding of Mexico often is not perceived as marking the beginning of national development. On the contrary, many assume that Mexico first had to overcome its "negative colonial heritage" in order to form a true "national" government.[9] Hence, most scholars consider Independence a step backward, an attempt to restore a colonial order which, presumably, the insurgents had sought to end.

The contrasting interpretations of the process of independence in the United States and in Mexico raise significant questions. While in Mexico the "oligarchy," lawyers, and other urban groups tend to be dismissed in favor of rural insurgents, in the United States great latifundistas and slave owners, lawyers, and merchants are often depicted as "radicals." Is it that historians are discussing two very different processes, or do the national prejudices of the two countries cause scholars to emphasize those aspects which their "patriotism" dictates? Why is it that in the United States it is acceptable to have founding fathers such as George Washington and Thomas Jefferson, who were "oligarchs," while in Mexico they must be "populist" leaders, such as the *curas* Hidalgo and Morelos?

The answers are complex, but in the case of Mexico, which is the subject of this volume, the autonomists—the true founding fathers of the nation—chose to obfuscate their role in order to oppose Emperor Agustín I. It was they who, in 1821–1822, elevated the insurgents, and particularly Hidalgo and Morelos, to the pedestal of founding fathers.[10]

[8]See, for example, María de la Luz Parcero, "El liberalismo triunfante y el surgimiento de la historia nacional," in *Investigaciones contemporáneas sobre historia de México: Memorias de la Tercera Reunión de Historiadores Mexicanos y Norteamericanos* (Mexico and Austin: UNAM, El Colegio de México, and University of Texas, 1971), 443–457. More recently, Samuel I. del Villar argued passionately against Alan Riding's notion that Mexicans lacked the "morality" necessary for democracy. Villar asserts that "fortunately, Mexico has been a firmly established republic since 1864, and it also has . . . a constitution deeply rooted in its history which truly reflects the national morality and commands the way to democracy." That constitution, the charter of 1917, according to Villar is grounded upon the "constitutional order" established by the Constitution of 1857. Missing in his discussion is the Constitution of 1824, which founded the nation. See Samuel I. del Villar, "Morality and Democracy in Mexico: Some Personal Reflections," in *Sucesión presidencial: The 1988 Mexican Presidential Elections*, ed. Edgar W. Butler and Jorge A. Bustamante (Boulder: Westview Press, 1991), 143–147.

[9]See, for example, Romeo Flores Caballero, *La contrarrevolución en la independencia: Los españoles en la vida política, social y económica de México, 1804–1838* (Mexico: El Colegio de México, 1969).

[10]Jaime E. Rodríguez O., "From Royal Subject to Republican Citizen: The Role of the Autonomists in the Independence of Mexico," in idem, ed., *The Independence of Mexico and the Creation of the New Nation* (Los Angeles: UCLA Latin American Center, 1989), 19–43; idem, "El *Bosquejo ligerísimo de la*

The notion that the rural insurgents (who lost) were the true founders of the nation, while the autonomists—the urban elites—(who won) were not, has become an obstacle to understanding Mexico's past. Instead of interpreting the country's political history as a process of evolutionary change, as is the case in the United States, historians of Mexico often dismiss the nation's first political structures and institutions as irrelevant, while seeking "revolutionary" transformations that, presumably, advanced the country's political development. The nature of rural movements and the aspirations of country people have become the leitmotif of Mexican history. Historiographical debates often concentrate on the role of campesinos.[11] For example, the current disagreements between "revisionists" and "traditionalists" about the nature of the Mexican Revolution generally turn on the role of "popular" rural groups in that great upheaval.[12]

The emphasis placed by many historians on agrarian issues has obscured the nature of the political process. By focusing on rural conflict, they have overlooked the importance of the relationship between the city and

---

revolución de Mégico de Vicente Rocafuerte," Paper prepared for the Seminario de Historiografía de México, Instituto de Investigaciones Históricas, UNAM, March 1992.

[11]The historiography of rural movements is quite extensive; see, for example, Virginia Guedea, "Alzamientos y motines," in *Historia de México*, ed. Miguel León-Portilla (Mexico: Editorial Salvat, 1974), 5:35–50; Enrique Florescano, *Origen y desarrollo de los problemas agrarios en México, 1500–1821* (Mexico: Editorial Era, 1976); William B. Taylor, *Drinking, Homicide, and Rebellion in Colonial Mexican Villages* (Stanford: Stanford University Press, 1979); José Luis Mirafuentes, *Movimientos de resistencia y rebeliones indígenas en el norte de México* (Mexico: UNAM, 1989); Felipe Castro Gutiérrez, *Movimientos populares en Nueva España: Michoacán, 1766–1767* (Mexico: UNAM, 1990); Leticia Reina, *Las rebeliones campesinas en México, 1819–1906* (Mexico: Siglo XXI, 1980); Miguel Mejía Fernández, *Política agraria en México en el siglo XIX* (Mexico: Siglo XXI, 1979); John Tutino, *From Insurrection to Revolution in Mexico: Social Bases of Agrarian Violence, 1750–1940* (Princeton: Princeton University Press, 1986); Friedrich Katz, ed., *Riot, Rebellion, and Revolution: Rural Social Conflict in Mexico* (Princeton: Princeton University Press, 1988); and Jaime E. Rodríguez O., ed., *Patterns of Contention in Mexican History* (Wilmington: Scholarly Resources, 1992). The Mexican Revolution has been interpreted by some as a classic rural movement; see, for example, Frank Tannenbaum, *The Mexican Agrarian Revolution* (New York: Macmillan Company, 1929); and Alan Knight, *The Mexican Revolution*, 2 vols. (Cambridge: Cambridge University Press, 1988).

[12]Alan Knight has championed the "populist" cause. See, for example, the exchanges between Knight and his critics at the Simposio de Historiografía Mexicanista held at Oaxtepec, Morelos, in October 1988. Alan Knight, "Interpretaciones recientes de la Revolución Mexicana"; Alicia Hernández Chávez, "Comentario"; Gloria Villegas Moreno, "Comentario"; and Javier Garcíadiego Dantán, "Revisionistas al paredón," in *Memorias del Simposio de Historiografía Mexicanista* (Mexico: Comité Mexicano de Ciencias Históricas, 1990), 193–221.

the countryside in Mexico. Although a predominantly agrarian society, the nation was a land dominated by cities and towns. Landowners, large and small, lived in urban areas, not on their estates. Similarly, Indians congregated in corporate villages. Political power at all levels, therefore, resided in urban centers. While insurgents often dominated much of the countryside, they could not win their struggle without support from the cities.

The development of social history in recent decades has emphasized the role of "popular" groups, particularly country people. Students of popular movements, however, frequently disregard "the problem of the difference between the masses, rural or urban, and those who led them." Moreover, as Virginia Guedea notes, "the victors [of many rural upheavals] have been city people. . . . And that is because, after all, political power resides principally in the capital cities, both in the states and in the nation."[13]

Although politics and political institutions existed in the colonial period, modern national politics emerged in 1808.[14] The theories, processes, institutions, and practices that would determine Mexico's political history emerged during the Independence era. They evolved, as José Miranda and Nettie Lee Benson have observed, from Hispanic traditions.[15] The deliberative juntas of 1808 initiated the new political process in New Spain.[16] Subsequently, the Spanish imperial crisis provided the opportunity for much greater participation when the peninsular government of national defense, the Junta Suprema Central, convened a cortes that enacted the Constitution of 1812. That charter dramatically expanded the possibilities for political participation by establishing representative government at the imperial, provincial, and local levels. Elections to the cortes, the provincial deputations, and the constitutional ayuntamientos offered New Spaniards

[13]Virginia Guedea, "En torno a la Independencia y la Revolución," in *The Revolutionary Process in Mexico: Essays on Political and Social Change, 1880–1940*, ed. Jaime E. Rodríguez O. (Los Angeles: UCLA Latin American Center Publications, 1990), 273.

[14]I am grateful to Virginia Guedea for information on the difference between colonial politics and the modern politics that emerged during the Independence period. Personal communication, November 23, 1989.

[15]See, for example, José Miranda, *Las ideas y las instituciones políticas mexicanas*, 2d ed. (Mexico: UNAM, 1978); Nettie Lee Benson, *La Diputación Provincial y el federalismo mexicano* (Mexico: El Colegio de México, 1955); and her "Spain's Contribution to Federalism in Mexico," in *Essays in Mexican History*, ed. Thomas E. Cotner and Carlos Castañeda (Austin: Institute of Latin American Studies, 1958), 90–103.

[16]The principal work on the 1808 crisis is Virginia Guedea, "Criollos y peninsulares en 1808: Dos puntos de vista sobre lo español" (Licenciatura thesis, Universidad Iberoamericana, 1964); and idem, "El golpe de Estado de 1808," *Universidad de México: Revista de la Universidad Nacional Autónoma de México* 488 (September 1991): 21–24.

opportunities for self-rule.[17] In ways we have yet to understand, political power was transferred from the center to the localities, as large numbers of people were incorporated into the political process. Because the constitution allowed cities and towns with a thousand or more citizens to form ayuntamientos and because it established neither property nor literacy qualifications for exercising political citizenship, the new charter introduced popular representative government. As a result, Mexico would experience mass politics from the outset.

After 1821 the newly independent Mexicans followed the precedents established by the Spanish constitutional system. The Mexican Constitution of 1824 not only was modeled on the Spanish charter but also repeated sections verbatim. Many state constitutions also followed the Spanish model. This was only natural, since many New Spaniards had served in the cortes and had participated in drafting the Spanish document.[18] Other processes and institutions, such as elections, the *jefes políticos*, the militia, and the courts, drew upon the precedents established by the Constitution of Cádiz.[19]

[17]On the new institutions and the new politics see Nettie Lee Benson, ed., *Mexico and the Spanish Cortes, 1810–1822* (Austin: University of Texas Press, 1966); Benson, *La Diputación Provincial*; and idem, "The Contested Mexican Election of 1812," *Hispanic American Historical Review* 26 (August 1946): 336–350; Virginia Guedea, "Las primeras elecciones populares en la ciudad de México, 1812–1813," *Mexican Studies/Estudios Mexicanos* 7, no. 1 (Winter 1991): 1–28; idem, *En busca de un gobierno alterno: Los Guadalupes de México* (Mexico: UNAM, 1992); and idem, "Los procesos electorales insurgentes," *Estudios de historia novohispana* 11 (1991): 201–249; and Rafael Alba, ed., *La Constitución de 1812 en la Nueva España*, 2 vols. (Mexico: Secretaría de Relaciones Exteriores, Imprenta Guerrero Hnos., 1912–1913).

[18]Jaime E. Rodríguez O., "Intellectuals and the Mexican Constitution of 1824," in *Los intelectuales y el poder en México*, ed. Roderic Ai Camp, Charles Hale, and Josefina Zoraida Vázquez (Mexico and Los Angeles: El Colegio de México and UCLA Latin American Center Publications, 1991), 63–74; and my essay "The Constitution of 1824 and the Formation of the Mexican State" in this volume.

[19]On elections consult Benson, "The Contested Mexican Election of 1812"; and idem, "Texas's Failure to Send a Deputy to the Spanish Cortes, 1810–1812," *Southwestern Historical Quarterly* 64 (July 1960): 1–22; Charles R. Berry, "The Election of Mexican Deputies to the Spanish Cortes, 1810–1822," in Benson, ed., *Mexico and the Spanish Cortes*, 10–42; Virginia Guedea, "The First Popular Elections in Mexico City, 1812–1813," in this volume; idem, "Procesos electorales insurgentes"; idem, "El pueblo de México y las elecciones de 1812," in *La ciudad de México en la primera mitad del siglo XIX*, 2 vols., ed. Regina Hernández Franyuti (Mexico: Instituto de Investigaciones Dr. José María Luis Mora, 1994), 2:125–165; Antonio Annino, "Practiche creole e liberalismo nella crisi dell spazio urbano coloniale: Il 29 de noviembre 1812 a Città del Messico," *Quaderni Storici* (69) 23, no. 3 (December 1988): 727–763; Michael P. Costeloe, "Generals versus Politicians: Santa Anna and the 1842 Congressional

During the next century the political processes and institutions of Mexico continued to evolve as its citizens sought to adapt the political system to their changing needs. Because the country experienced economic depression, political instability, and military defeat in the nineteenth century, it has been easy to assume that "inherent flaws" in the earlier political structures had to be overcome in order to achieve "success." Thus, some scholars have viewed the Reform, the Porfiriato, the Revolution, the "revolutionary" regimes, and current reform movements as the solutions to the nation's "problems." In short, the tendency has been to interpret Mexican history as a series of breaks with the past.[20]

Yet, as I have argued elsewhere, "change is sequential and does not advance by leaps."[21] If we are to understand Mexico's political history, we need to study its "evolution," its "development," its "growth." The

---

Elections in Mexico," *Bulletin of Latin American Research* 8, no. 2 (1980): 257–274. On the *jefes políticos* see Romana Falcón, "Jefes políticos y rebeliones campesinas: Uso y abuso del poder en el Estado de México," in Rodríguez, *Patterns of Contention*, 243–273. On the militia see Alicia Hernández Chávez, "La Guardia Nacional y movilización política de los pueblos," in Rodríguez, *Patterns of Contention*, 207–225; and Pedro Santoni, "A Fear of the People: The Civic Militia of Mexico in 1845," *Hispanic American Historical Review* 68, no. 2 (May 1988): 269–288.

[20]Here I do not mean to imply that scholars have not studied the nation's political processes. On the contrary, some distinguished works have been written; see, for example, Guedea, *En busca de un gobierno alterno*; Benson, *La Diputación Provincial*; Javier Ocampo, *Las ideas de un día: El pueblo mexicano ante la consumación de su Independencia* (Mexico: El Colegio de México, 1969); Andrés Lira, *Comunidades indígenas frente a la ciudad de México: Tenochtitlan y Tlatelolco, sus pueblos y barrios, 1812–1919* (Zamora: El Colegio de Michoacán, 1983); Charles Macune, *El Estado de México y la federación mexicana* (Mexico: Fondo de Cultura Económica, 1978); Michael P. Costeloe, *La Primera República Federal de México, 1824–1835* (Mexico: Fondo de Cultura Económica, 1975); Barbara A. Tenenbaum, *The Politics of Penury: Debts and Taxes in Mexico, 1821–1856* (Albuquerque: University of New Mexico Press, 1986); Cecilia Noriega Elío, *El Constituyente de 1842* (Mexico: UNAM, 1986); Daniel Cosío Villegas, *La Constitución de 1857 y sus críticos* (Mexico: SEP, 1973); Walter V. Scholes, *Mexican Politics during the Juárez Regime, 1855–1872* (Columbia: University of Missouri Press, 1957); Daniel Cosío Villegas, ed., *Historia moderna de México*, 10 vols. (Mexico: Editorial Hermes, 1955–1972); Laurens Ballard Perry, *Juárez and Díaz: Machine Politics in Mexico* (DeKalb: Northern Illinois University Press, 1978); Knight, *Mexican Revolution*; and François-Xavier Guerra, *Le Mexique: De l'Ancien Régime à la Révolution*, 2 vols. (Paris: L'Harmattan, 1985), to name only some that come to mind. Of course, there are many political studies of the Revolution and the later twentieth century.

[21]Jaime E. Rodríguez O., "La historiografía de la Primera República," in *Memorias del Simposio de Historiografía Mexicanista* (Mexico: Comité Mexicano de Ciencias Históricas, 1990), 147.

advantage of such an approach is that it allows scholars to understand "what ended, what began, and what continued," not only as a result of Independence but also throughout the nation's independent history.[22]

The essays in this volume examine some of the politics, processes, and institutions of Mexico during the first half of the nineteenth century. Christon I. Archer's "Politicization of the Army of New Spain during the War of Independence, 1810–1821," examines the process by which the army became a powerful force in independent Mexico. He argues that in order to overcome the insurgency, the royal army developed a counterinsurgency program that created a series of decentralized units. In the process, the officers introduced military rule in New Spain. Commanders governed their regions as they wished, often overruling civilian authorities and enriching themselves in the process. But with the restoration of the Spanish Constitution in 1820, "the military temporarily lost the dominance that for years permitted soldiers to control Mexican politics." Ultimately, the officers opted to support Iturbide's Plan de Iguala and Independence. As a result, they remained a pivotal factor in national politics.

In her essay "The First Popular Elections in Mexico City, 1812–1813," Virginia Guedea analyzes the significance of the new political processes introduced by the Constitution of 1812. She argues that "the elections . . . notably affected the process of emancipation because they offered New Spaniards seeking change an alternative to the armed insurrection." They provided the people of New Spain with the possibility of widespread political participation and representative government, an opportunity taken up by large sectors of the population, including the Indians and the *castas*. The elections also demonstrated the great desire which New Spaniards possessed for home rule. As a result, "the electoral model established by the Constitution of 1812 did not end with independence from Spain but continued during the early years of the new nation."

My essay, "The Constitution of 1824 and the Formation of the Mexican State," carries the examination of the new political system into the 1820s. It traces the amazing growth of political participation during those years and the emergence of a strong sense of nationality among the people of Mexico. The work highlights the continuities between the Spanish charter and the Mexican Constitution of 1824. "Events in Mexico," however, led to the framing of "a constitution to meet the unique circumstances of the nation. The principal innovations—republicanism, federalism, and a presidency—were adopted to address Mexico's new reality."

In "The Making of a Fait Accompli: Mexico and the Provincias Internas, 1776–1846," Barbara A. Tenenbaum argues that the North deliberately chose to remain a part of the new nation. She observes that the

[22]Doris Ladd, *The Mexican Nobility at Independence, 1780–1826* (Austin: Institute of Latin American Studies, University of Texas, 1976), 170.

region developed its own economic, military, and political structure, which often functioned independently of the center. As a result, the area could have separated from Mexico and become an independent country, as occurred in the viceroyalties of South America. She indicates that, contrary to generally accepted views, "the residents of the Provincias Internas demonstrated substantial loyalty to the nation during the period from 1776 to 1846. . . . Far from being a drain on the imperial or national coffers . . . , the *norteños* actually provided more succor [to the nation] than their counterparts in most other areas." And she concludes that "it is now time for a thorough examination of how such loyalty evolved."

The essays in this book examine aspects of Mexico's political process during the first half of the nineteenth century. All emphasize the internal and evolutionary nature of political change in Mexico. As a group, the authors of these essays are revisionists; that is, they challenge traditional interpretations of events and demonstrate the complexity of Mexico's political processes and institutions. While illuminating key aspects of the nation's political system, the essays also indicate how much there is still left to learn about the country's political history.

Politicization of the Army of New Spain during the War of Independence, 1810–1821

Christon I. Archer

> Ya no es posible Exmo. Señor sufrir más de esta vil canalla y
> solo un exemplarisimo terror ha de hacer entrarles en su deber.

Brigadier José de la Cruz[1]

AFTER ONLY TWO MONTHS of fighting the popular rebellion launched by Father Miguel Hidalgo, frontline army commanders such as Brigadier José de la Cruz demanded extreme solutions. Scattering insurgent forces, cursing the perversity of Mexican rebel priests, and ready to execute anyone caught with weapons in their hands, Cruz's royalist columns reoccupied towns and villages on the strategic route between Mexico City and Querétaro. Following a forced march, on November 21, 1810, they assaulted the rebel town of Huichapan. In the distance, 150 to 200 insurgent cavalry dispersed precipitously and could be seen in full flight heading for the mountains. Frightened by rumors that they would be treated to royalist vengeance of blood and fire, the Indian populace fled to the sanctuary of the parish church tower. The remainder of the community made an obsequious show of friendship and welcomed the troops with displays of fireworks and other acts to demonstrate their abject fealty.[2] Behind this facade of loyalty, Cruz liberated nine *gachupín* (European Spanish) merchants from Mexico City, Chihuahua, and Querétaro who had been confined under harsh conditions in

---

[1]José de la Cruz to Viceroy Francisco Xavier de Venegas, Huichapan, November 28, 1810, Archivo General de la Nación, Mexico City, Ramo de Operaciones de Guerra (hereafter cited as AGN:OG), vol. 141.

[2]Cruz to Venegas, Huichapan, November 21, 1810, AGN:OG, vol. 141.

the town jail. Four of these men suffered grave injuries; they included Manuel Yzcoa, a retired militia captain and Mexico City merchant, who died of his wounds three days later.[3] Enraged by Cruz's reports of rebels who were said to have trussed up royalist soldiers and run them through with lances and also by news that two hundred loyalists had been executed in cold blood at the Guanajuato jail, Viceroy Francisco Xavier de Venegas informed Cruz that the authors of the insurrection should be put to death by being "fried in oil."[4]

As *comandante general* of the Army of the Right, Cruz moved quickly to establish the supremacy of the military over the civil administration. At Querétaro, Celaya, Valladolid, and finally at his command in Guadalajara for the duration of the war until 1821, Cruz exercised extremely broad powers and often challenged the wartime viceroys. Arriving in Mexico from Spain at the beginning of the Hidalgo Revolt, Cruz argued that the only way to stamp out rebellion was through the steady application of avenging force. At Querétaro in December 1810, Cruz dispensed arbitrary justice to 460 rebel prisoners in the city jails who were awaiting trials and sentences for crimes connected with rebellion.[5] Some had accepted military commissions from Hidalgo or served as sergeants, corporals, or soldiers in the insurgent forces. Cruz sentenced many of them to death and then ordered their bodies displayed as what he termed salutary reminders to the rest of the populace that rebellion did not pay.[6] At Acámbaro on Christmas Day 1810, he condemned sixteen rebel prisoners to be executed by firing squads and ordered their bloody remains to be hung up in fours at each of the principal entries to the town.[7]

Cruz's mistrust of the Mexican population and his willingness to implement draconian punishments to suppress future rebellion became even more extreme on December 29 when his army entered the city of Valladolid (Morelia). Although there was much pealing of church bells, cheering from fawning crowds, and a formal Te Deum celebrated at the city cathedral, Cruz

---

[3]Noticia de los Europeos que a mi llegada a este pueblo existían presos, José de la Cruz, November 24, 1810, AGN:OG, vol. 141.

[4]Venegas to Cruz, November 28, 1810, AGN:OG, vol. 141.

[5]Cruz to Venegas, Querétaro, December 19, 1810, AGN:OG, vol. 142.

[6]Cruz to Venegas, Querétaro, December 16, 1810, AGN, Sección de Historia, vol. 106. Cruz met at Querétaro with Auditor Matías de los Ríos, who agreed that shortcuts were necessary in normal peacetime legal procedures so that the accused rebels could be brought to justice. Cruz planned to deal with all cases against accused rebels within three or four days. He expressed annoyance that a number of the most prominent prisoners—even the corregidor, who was considered one of the major conspirators—had been released due to their high social class.

[7]Cruz to Calleja, Acámbaro, December 25, 1810, AGN:OG, vol. 140; Cruz to Venegas, December 25, 1810, AGN:OG, vol. 142.

was in no mood to believe the sincerity of "these perfidious inhabitants." He grumbled to Félix María Calleja, commander of the Army of the Center, that the celebration welcoming the royalist forces was not nearly as solemn as when the city received Father Hidalgo.[8] Aware that the royalists were about to enter the city, remaining cabildo members liberated 170 bedraggled European Spaniards who had been incarcerated under harsh conditions in city monasteries. Before entering the city, Cruz issued public orders to the commander of his vanguard that if the plebeians of Valladolid killed any more Europeans, he would put to the sword the whole population— exempting only women and children. As might be expected, the liberated *gachupines* embraced Cruz and his soldiers, shouting "¡Viva el Rey, vivan nuestros libertadores!"[9]

The chilling reports of survivors of massacres in cold blood of innocent fathers and husbands drained the royalist officers of any lingering humane sentiments. During the rebel occupation, small groups of *gachupines* had been removed from the prisons in irons and marched to secluded locations in the countryside where their throats were cut. Stripped of all assets, the survivors of these victims lived in poverty and had to beg in the streets. What was worse, the rebels refused to inform the families of executed Spaniards about their true fate. When rumors of the killings circulated, the rebels not only refused the families the right to grieve but also went so far as to threaten them with the death penalty if they complained or disapproved of the atrocities.[10]

Like many other army commanders, Cruz blamed the criollo clergy for legitimizing rebellion and for organizing the towns that joined Hidalgo. In his view, the curates and priests convinced the people that the rebel cause was just and even went so far as to use the confessional to spread "these detestable maxims." The renewed pretense of loyalty at Valladolid did not deceive Cruz for a moment. He estimated that a majority in the city continued secretly to support the rebels. Almost two-thirds of the Valladolid population had fled to seek refuge from royalist vengeance, and much of the

[8]Cruz to Calleja, December 28, 1810, AGN:OG, vol. 143.

[9]Cruz to Venegas, December 29, 1810, AGN:OG, vol. 142; Cruz to Félix Calleja, Hacienda de Goleta, December 27, 1810, AGN:OG, vol. 140. At first, Cruz planned to enter Valladolid on December 28. Even as the royalist army approached, plebeian elements led by a Toluca blacksmith named Tomás (called El Anglo-Americano) formed a mob that killed three gachupines. See Cabildo of Valladolid to Cruz, December 26, 1810, AGN:OG, vol. 140; and Lucas Alamán, *Historia de México desde los primeros movimientos que prepararon su independencia en el año de 1808 hasta la época presente* (Mexico: Fondo de Cultura Económica, 1985), 2:73-74.

[10]Ibid. Also see Brian R. Hamnett, "Royalist Counterinsurgency and the Continuity of Rebellion: Guanajuato and Michoacán, 1813–1820," *Hispanic American Historical Review* 62, no. 1 (February 1982): 23.

urban leadership escaped to Guadalajara where they joined the insurgent command. The question for Cruz was how far to purge the city of its traditional ruling class. He considered banishing all of the four hundred regular and secular clergymen, transferring the untrustworthy militia units out of the province, and disbanding the city government.[11] The Michoacán militias stood out for their treachery and willingness to embrace the rebel cause. Even if the senior officers were not inherently disloyal, they had failed to resist the uprising or to provide examples for their troops. Major Manuel Gallegos of the Infantería Provincial de Valladolid spent the two months of rebel occupation hiding at the home of a loyal ecclesiastic. Colonel Francisco Menocal and Major Rafael Ortega[12] of the Dragones de Pátzcuaro simply disappeared quietly to their haciendas. When Cruz reoccupied Valladolid, they reappeared, claiming chronic illnesses and making a variety of other excuses. Menocal, a wealthy hacendado who owned estates and properties at Pátzcuaro and Zamora, was in his early sixties and might not have been robust enough to lead his troops into combat. More likely, however, as with many other militia officers and criollo leaders of Michoacán, where necessary he cooperated with the insurgents and where possible he distanced himself from the conflict.[13]

In his investigation of the military collapse at Valladolid, Viceroy Venegas could not explain the disastrous failure of a garrison of one thousand men commanded by trained officers and supported by four artillery pieces. If this force had stood its ground, Venegas believed that Hidalgo's poorly trained and ill-equipped rebels could not have occupied the city. While the viceroy had not heard about Colonel Menocal's alleged disabilities, he concluded that the defensive operations had not been conducted by decisive and honorable commanders. He dismissed Major Gallegos as an officer who lacked energy and military ardor. The inescapable conclusion was that the existing provincial militia units of Michoacán had not lived up to minimum expectations and would have to be thoroughly reformed.[14] Although royalist informers implicated members of the Valladolid cabildo and other administrators who had assisted the rebel occupation, Cruz knew that the repression and punishment of all guilty

[11]Cruz to Venegas, December 30, 1810, AGN:OG, vol. 142.

[12]By 1814, Ortega had recovered his reputation and was *teniente coronel graduado* and *sargento mayor* of the Regimiento de Dragones de Moncada. See Juan Ruíz de Apodaca to Pascual de Liñan, September 11, 1818, AGN:OG, vol. 485.

[13]Cruz to Venegas, Valladolid, December 29, 1810, AGN:OG, vol. 142. For information on the Michoacán militias see Christon I. Archer, *The Army in Bourbon Mexico, 1760–1810* (Albuquerque: University of New Mexico Press, 1977), 162–163 and 212. Although he was born in Cuba, Menocal identified himself with Mexican criollo interests.

[14]Venegas to Cruz, December 31, 1810, AGN:OG, vol. 142.

Mexicans was not a practicable option. It was one thing to lose confidence in the loyalty of Mexicans but quite another to find alternatives to govern the country. In many instances, Cruz and other royalist commanders could not find trustworthy persons to reconstitute the urban administrations, collect taxes, and staff the royalist regime. At Valladolid, Cruz lamented that the only men he trusted without reservation were those who had family connections in Mexico City or Spain. At the same time, the royalists discovered quickly that ongoing purges, trials, and executions prevented renewed production in industry, mining, agriculture, and commerce.[15]

Like Calleja and other royalist commanders, Cruz concluded that sanguinary repression was not the right answer to restoring peace. If cities and provinces were to be returned to productivity, former insurgents had to be amnestied as soon as possible after the royalists reasserted their control.[16] Moreover, military commanders could not assume all of the duties and responsibilities of the civilian regime. Working long hours and receiving a constant flood of petitions from the Valladolid public, Cruz discovered that civilian politics left him totally exhausted. As he informed Calleja, "This is a dog's life: they don't leave me for a moment and I am becoming more and more weary."[17] In his view the one way to destroy the germ of evil behind the rebellion was to assign small army units to scour all districts of the province and thereby regain the loyalty of the inhabitants.[18]

As military *comandante general* of Nueva Galicia and *presidente* of the Audiencia from 1811 to 1821, Cruz emerged as something of a prototype for the provincial caudillo. He pursued a multifaceted counterinsurgency war, mobilized the western provinces of New Spain, and controlled every aspect of society and the economy. His heavy-handed military administration overshadowed the civilian bureaucracy and governed royalist Jalisco for a decade of continuous conflict against guerrilla warfare. With the perimeters of his command and especially the south solidly in insurgent hands, Cruz conceived a strategy based upon mobile cavalry divisions that could reach out to combat a rebellion "that renews itself and grows like grass."[19] He criticized other royalist commanders and even his own subordinates such as Brigadier Torcuato Trujillo, who commanded Valladolid province, for their inflexibility and dependence upon static defenses. Rather than deploying mobile divisions to pursue guerrilla bands and to prevent the possible

---

[15]Cruz to Venegas, December 31, 1810, AGN:OG, vol. 142. Cruz asked the viceroy to send trustworthy persons who could help to reestablish the provincial government.

[16]Calleja to Cruz, Guanajuato, December 5, 1810, AGN:OG, vol. 140. Calleja expressed concern about the patriotic zeal of Cruz in punishing the population.

[17]Cruz to Calleja, December 28, 1810, AGN:OG, vol. 143.

[18]Cruz to Venegas, January 2, 1811, AGN:OG, vol. 146.

[19]Cruz to Calleja, September 2, 1811, AGN:OG, vol. 145.

coalescence of insurgent armies, Trujillo tied down his garrison in defense of the city of Valladolid. Cruz criticized this approach to insurgency and argued that the full pacification of Michoacán might require the deaths of twenty thousand to thirty thousand rebels. Providing an example of aggressive counterinsurgency, in 1811 between August 21 and September 2, Cruz's divisions in Nueva Galicia killed more than eight hundred rebels.[20]

While Trujillo was no different from Cruz in his goal to crush rebellion, he suffered a weakness that was common among European officers who served in Mexico. He favored his *gachupín* cronies and was distrustful of others around him who might have been his allies. On many occasions, Trujillo engaged in quarrels with his criollo officers and civilian administrators that almost erupted into brawls. In one incident, he sentenced the *administrador de tabaco* at Pátzcuaro to eight days' public confinement with his head and feet in the stocks. The intendant of Valladolid, Manuel Merino, conceded that while Trujillo might be a good soldier, he lacked entirely "the qualities of a prudent politician."[21] The officers, soldiers, ecclesiastics, and honorable residents of Valladolid suffered from Trujillo's public humiliations, insulting behavior, and accusations of disloyalty. (In the end these indiscriminate attacks would bring him down. In 1813, Bishop-elect Manuel Abad y Queipo and the religious and secular cabildos of Valladolid would convince Viceroy Calleja that Trujillo's tyrannical methods and corruption were more than sufficient grounds for his dismissal.[22])

[20]Ibid. For information on the controversial Torcuato Trujillo see Alámán, *Historia de México*, 2:78. Trujillo was later relieved of his command for "impetuous behavior." Calleja was said to have described him as "a madman with a sword." In part, Trujillo appears to have possessed the prejudices of European Spaniards against Mexican criollos. At his house and in public, he described royalist officers as "cowards" and "thieves." Even worse, Trujillo wrote letters condemning the military ability of his fellow commanders. He said that José de la Cruz, officers of Calleja's Army of the Center, and other senior commanders sacrificed their troops to protect their own personal ambitions. See, for example, Ramón Díaz de Ortega to Calleja, Guanajuato, August 14, 1811; Manuel Espinosa Tello to Calleja, Guanajuato, August 16, 1811; Miguel del Campo to Calleja, Guanajuato, October 10, 1811; and José María Echeagaray to Calleja, Acámbaro, December 2, 1811, AGN:OG, vol. 181.

[21]Juan Diez to Calleja, Acámbaro, December 5, 1811; Manuel Merino to Callejo, December 26, 1811; AGN:OG, vol. 181.

[22]Alamán, *Historia de México*, 3:380–381. Although Viceroy Calleja ordered Trujillo to remain in New Spain when his mentor Venegas returned to Europe, the charges were not fully investigated and he was able to go back to the continent. At Valladolid, Diego García Conde reversed Trujillo's approaches to defense. He organized mobile army divisions and recruited *compañías territoriales* under Calleja's counterinsurgency plan. See García Conde to Calleja, Valladolid, May 16, 1813; and Calleja to García Conde, June 12, 1813, AGN:OG, vol. 900.

Although Cruz was careful to maintain the confidence of his military commanders, civilian administrators, and royalist elements among the Guadalajara populace, he was heavy-handed and arbitrary in some of his policies. To identify civilian noncombatants, he ordered all urban and rural residents, no matter what their class, to wear a red badge or cockade on their hats to signify their support for the royalist cause. At the same time, he outlawed garments made from printed cotton that in the past had been called *cotón americano* and now *cotón insurgente* because it was worn by many of the rebel bands. He stressed that common cotton cloth used by the poor classes and workers as their normal dress was quite different from *cotón insurgente*, which stood out for its designs.[23] Moreover, the rough justice of Cruz's flying-column cavalry expeditions into rural districts of Nueva Galicia probably created new centers of rebellion rather than advanced pacification. By 1813, Indian rebels of the Lake Chapala region fortified the Isla de Mezcala and dominated districts surrounding the lake. In the first of many disastrous clashes at Chapala, Cruz lost one of his most active counterinsurgency commanders, Lieutenant Colonel Angel Linares, five officers, and twenty-three infantrymen. While the lieutenant colonel was conducting an unauthorized reconnaissance by boat of the Mezcala island fortifications, a rebel flotilla of seventy canoes surrounded and captured Linares and his men, who were executed at the village of Tizapán.[24]

Distraught by the loss of Linares, pressured by insurgent successes, and convinced that he could not manage war in an enormous region that included the provinces of Guanajuato and Valladolid, Cruz requested Viceroy Venegas to decentralize his command. In a personal note he criticized the viceroy for expecting a military miracle in Nueva Galicia without making available the proper assistance. Cruz complained: "Can I make the rocks give me muskets, pistols, swords, and powder?"[25] He proposed that Venegas should separate Guanajuato and Valladolid provinces from the Nueva Galicia command and reinforce them with troops and arms. Cruz argued that cavalry, the essential military arm to suppress insurgents who used guerrilla warfare, must be equipped with swords and pistols. Mexican troopers absolutely abhorred the lance, which in many units was their only weapon. Swords manufactured in Guadalajara cost too much and were absolutely useless—the blades were so brittle that they broke in the scabbard during ordinary movements of the horse and rider.[26] In his search for better weapons, Cruz dispatched an agent, Captain Manuel Peñuñuri, to Mexico City, but he was

[23]Bando de José de la Cruz, Guadalajara, July 25, 1811, AGN:OG, vol. 145.
[24]Cruz to Venegas, February 27, 1813, AGN:OG, vol. 149. See Antonio de Alba, *Chapala* (Guadalajara: Publicaciones del Banco Industrial de Jalisco, 1954), 90.
[25]Ibid. Cruz attached a personal note to the official dispatch.
[26]Cruz to Venegas, February 27, 1813, AGN:OG, vol. 149.

unable to obtain either arms or additional supplies of gunpowder for Nueva Galicia.[27]

After he became viceroy on March 4, 1813, Calleja reorganized the military command structure to address the different challenges to the royalist cause. While the army had not suffered major defeats, it was divided and subdivided into small divisions that garrisoned towns and districts throughout the country. Many units lacked adequate weapons, and some divisions were so deeply in debt that soldiers were paid months in arrears. As a result of these factors, high desertion levels affected almost all royalist units, including the recently arrived Spanish expeditionary battalions. In the south, the insurgent leader José María Morelos recovered from the defeat at Cuautla Amilpas in May 1812, raised a new army of fourteen thousand to sixteen thousand men, and reequipped his forces with muskets and sixty artillery pieces.[28] By December the rebels occupied Oaxaca and extended their sway coast to coast across New Spain and southward to Guatemala. Insurgent forces threatened communications with Veracruz and raided the tobacco-producing districts of Córdoba and Orizaba. While the military situation to the north of the capital was somewhat less menacing, guerrilla forces continued to interdict commerce between the capital and the strategic distribution point of Querétaro. Calleja knew very well that without silver convoys from the northern mining districts, the regime would not be able to pay the royalist garrisons of Mexico City and the province of Puebla or meet the multitude of demands upon the wartime treasury.

Given this strategic situation, Calleja implemented a plan to create strong regional centers of royalist military power that would match the insurgents. Although historians often link Calleja's 1811 Reglamento Político Militar[29] with his 1813 decentralization plan, the new approach was both strategic and tactical in its orientation and goals. With the threat of Morelos from Oaxaca, the first task was to unite the different royalist

---

[27]Cruz to Venegas, March 4, 18, 1813, AGN:OG, vol. 149. Cruz asked for 1,500 muskets, 600 pairs of pistols, 1,500 swords, officers, and a European battalion.

[28]Calleja to Minister of War, March 15, 1813, Archivo General de las Indias, Sección de México, legajo 1322.

[29]Reglamento político militar que deberán observar bajo las penas que señala los pueblos, haciendas, y ranchos a quienes se comunique por las autoridades legítimas y respectivas . . . , Aguascalientes, June 8, 1811, AGN:OG, vol. 186. Also see Christon I. Archer, " 'La Causa Buena': The Counterinsurgency Army of New Spain and the Ten Years' War," in *The Independence of Mexico and the Creation of the New Nation*, ed. Jaime E. Rodríguez O. (Los Angeles: UCLA Latin American Center Publications, 1989), 96–97; Hugh M. Hamill, Jr., "Royalist Counterinsurgency in the Mexican War for Independence: The Lessons of 1811," *Hispanic American Historical Review* 53, no. 3 (August 1973): 478–480; and Hamnett, "Royalist Counterinsurgency, 1813–1820," 24–26.

divisions in the province of Puebla under one powerful military chief who was also the governor. The objective was to form an Army of the South that was strong enough to engage Morelos, protect the tobacco districts, and support the armed commercial convoys between Mexico City and Veracruz. Calleja appointed Field Marshal Conde de Castro Terreño[30] to command Puebla with Brigadier Juan José Olazabal[31] as his subordinate. Within the Puebla commandancy, each district was to raise *compañías territoriales* (local militias) and fortify its towns with trenches and blockhouses to forestall the incursions of lightly armed insurgents. Although Calleja proposed to form a similar regional command with headquarters at Guanajuato or Querétaro, this plan depended upon the successful organization of Puebla, which at the time was the most important zone of combat.[32] Indeed, Calleja transferred much of the Mexico City garrison to Puebla and depleted the few royalist units available to support the provinces of Valladolid, Guanajuato, and Nueva Galicia.

In his plans for the west and north, Calleja adopted Cruz's argument to Venegas that Nueva Galicia was too large for a single military jurisdiction. To govern Guanajuato, he considered Colonel Pedro Celestino Negrete,[33] one of Cruz's most effective division commanders on the Chapala front, but later changed his mind to assign Lieutenant Colonel Agustín de Iturbide[34] as *comandante general* of the Tropas del Bajío y Provincia de Guanajuato.[35] To replace the rancorous Trujillo at Valladolid, Calleja appointed Brigadier Diego García Conde,[36] an old veteran of the prewar army of New Spain, who in 1810 had been captured and imprisoned by the rebels on his way to

[30]Although he did not have a specific posting, Castro Terreño had come to Mexico in 1811 from Cádiz with the Regimiento de Infantería de América.

[31]Olazabal was *ayudante mayor* of the army of New Spain and a division commander in the Province of Puebla. He had come to Mexico in 1811 as commander of the first battalion of the Regimiento de Infantería de América.

[32]For a detailed study see Brian R. Hamnett, *Roots of Insurgency: Mexican Regions, 1750–1824* (Cambridge, England: Cambridge University Press, 1986), 150–177.

[33]Negrete was a former junior naval officer who emerged as a senior royalist commander of the army of New Spain and later joined Agustín de Iturbide.

[34]A criollo, Iturbide joined the Mexican provincial army in 1797 and served in the cantonments and encampments of the Valladolid and Tula units. Following the outbreak of the Hidalgo Revolt, he became known for his zeal and effectiveness in combat.

[35]Instrucción para la División de la Provincia de Guanajuato, April 27, 1813; Iturbide to Calleja, Irapuato, May 28, 1813, AGN:OG, vol. 426.

[36]An ambitious but not always successful officer, García Conde began his military career in the blockade of Gibraltar. By 1810 he had served thirty-eight years in the army, most of which were with the Dragones de México. He was quartermaster of the cantonments during pre-1810 invasion threats and was anxious to become the intendant of a Mexican province. García Conde's ambitions resulted in part from the fact that he had six children to support.

take up the post of *comandante de armas* at Valladolid. These regional commanders were to work in concert with Cruz at Guadalajara and with the *comandantes de armas* at Querétaro, San Luis Potosí, and Zacatecas. Perhaps concerned by the potential dangers of concentrating so much military and political power in the regions, Calleja stressed that the provincial intendants (or corregidor in the case of Querétaro) and existing administrators of the Hacienda Pública were to retain their offices under the direction of the Gobierno Superior and Tribunales in Mexico City.[37] As might be expected, however, the civil authorities lacked the power to defend their prerogatives and their peacetime links with the central regime in the capital. Over time, they failed to prevent the regional army commanders from decentralizing the country into a series of semiautonomous and autonomous military satrapies.

From Guadalajara, Comandante General Cruz engaged in a spirited power struggle with Viceroy Calleja. Although he had recommended decentralization of his enormous command, he was shocked when Calleja actually moved to detach the provinces of Valladolid and Guanajuato from Nueva Galicia. In a self-deprecating letter written in his own hand, Cruz complained that the diminution of his powers must mean that he had fallen out of favor. Playing the consummate prima donna, he asked to be relieved of his duties as soon as possible and transferred back to Spain.[38] Cruz vented his frustrations about shortages of arms and fears that Morelos would sweep up the Pacific coast, invade Nueva Galicia through Colima, and then repeat the horror story that had led to the royalist loss of Oaxaca. Cruz reminded Calleja that even in the darkest days of its own national crisis, Spain had managed to dispatch army officers, weapons, and several thousand soldiers to reinforce Mexico. He could not believe that the Crown intended this assistance to be deployed only for the protection of the capital.[39]

Calleja sought to mollify Cruz and to let him know that the separation of Guanajuato and Valladolid from the Nueva Galicia command was not in any way meant as personal criticism. He reminded Cruz that the royalist military situation was worse in other provinces than in Nueva Galicia and suggested that exaggerated rumors should not be permitted to damage good relations between senior commanders. Calleja pointed out that while the main forces of Morelos were 250 leagues from Guadalajara, they threatened Taxco only 25 leagues from the capital. As for the Spanish expeditionary battalions, Calleja explained that they were garrisoned from Texas to the frontier of Oaxaca. He expressed mild amusement at Cruz's belief that the European forces had been deployed simply to protect the capital. Speaking sarcastically, Calleja thought this might not be such a bad idea. He explained to Cruz that "the capital is the place where one finds the enemy

---

[37]Calleja to his commanders, April 22, 1813, AGN:OG, vol. 149.
[38]Cruz to Calleja, May 12, 1813, AGN:OG, vol. 149.
[39]Cruz to Calleja, May 14, June 7, 1813, AGN:OG, vol. 149.

closest and with the only force capable of inspiring fears. Through its corruption and infinity of partisans within, it [Mexico City] offers a great field for their expectations and designs."[40] In conclusion, Calleja reminded Cruz that as viceroy he had to consider the military needs of all New Spain and not just of one region such as Nueva Galicia.

These were fine sentiments, but Cruz had his hands full with the insurgents of Mezcala and the littoral of Lake Chapala. For years they had embarrassed and baffled the better-armed royalists. Reconnaissance of the island fortifications by a newly constructed armed launch and five boats to prepare for a major assault scheduled for June 7, 1813, took place in a hail of musketry and cannon fire that killed three royalist soldiers and wounded twelve.[41] The amphibious assault led by Colonel Negrete was an even worse disaster. Negrete received wounds to his head and legs and contusions on his hand, and he lost the ends of two fingers. Six other officers suffered injuries and a naval pilot was killed by a musket shot. At least twenty soldiers died, forty were dealt life-threatening wounds, and another ninety received less severe injuries.[42] With his army deficient in experienced soldiers, Cruz had to contemplate the difficult mission of sealing off the shoreline of Lake Chapala and of constructing a massive floating artillery battery to besiege the Mezcala fortress. This latter project required twelve hundred heavy beams, cables, artillery, munitions, and other equipment from the San Blas naval base.[43] As if to underscore the marine side of the Chapala campaign, royalist sailors and oarsmen serving the fleet of boats blockading the rebel fortress contracted scurvy and suffered terribly from mange and other skin diseases.

Construction of the floating platform and of a fleet of assault boats delayed Cruz's plans to extinguish Mezcala and allowed many Indian guerrilla bands to operate in the rugged country south of Lake Chapala. By March 1814, however, Cruz visited the lakeside army encampment at Tlachichilco to inspect the troops that were to attack the island and to view the recently completed artillery platform. Much to his surprise, once the builders loaded the cannon, munitions, cables, and other equipment, there was space aboard for only about 100 soldiers. The original plans had called for a complement of 250 to 300 troops who would disembark to assault the rebel island. To make matters worse, during shakedown cruises the platform became unstable when fully loaded and was difficult to navigate. The eight boats designated to transport royalist soldiers had a limited maximum capacity of 134 men, which meant that the landing force could not total

[40]Calleja to Cruz, July 6, 1813, AGN:OG, vol. 149.
[41]Cruz to Calleja, June 7, 1813, AGN:OG, vol. 149.
[42]Cruz to Calleja, June 8, 1813, AGN:OG, vol. 149.
[43]Cruz to Calleja, November 16, 1813, AGN:OG, vol. 149.

more than 234 soldiers, including officers.[44] Against such well-constructed fortifications and rebel defenders "who are well known for their ferocity and barbarism," Cruz and Negrete believed that the Mezcala invasion force required at least 500 to 700 soldiers. Hastily convened meetings with naval officers examined the possibility of building additional rafts to convey 250 to 300 troops, but in the end the experts recommended the construction of a great barge at the naval yard in San Blas. This vessel would be built in frame and freighted overland to Lake Chapala, where timber suitable for marine construction was not available.

In the meantime, Cruz's problems at Lake Chapala continued to absorb an inordinate amount of his time and resources. Although the army anchored the floating battery off Mezcala and commenced day-and-night bombardment of the rebel fortifications, there were no signs of an early surrender. Before long, wave action and strong winds on the lake opened the seams of the floating battery and caused it to take on water. To prevent the platform from sinking, it had to be withdrawn from the blockade and stripped of its artillery, munitions, and equipment. Cruz convened a new junta of naval and army officers to recommend solutions. The marine builder argued that the floating platform had been constructed for only one *golpe de mano* and it was not able to resist the continuous wind and wave action on Lake Chapala that he equated to ocean conditions. Because of the nature of construction, it was impossible either to pump out the bilge or to careen the hull. Moreover, the softwood timbers had deteriorated so badly that repairs were estimated to cost as much as replacing the platform. This left the royalists with only four boats to blockade Mezcala, which was resupplied daily by a flotilla of over 250 Indian canoes.[45] The costly siege continued until November 1816, when the royalists finally closed the land and naval blockades, thus starving the insurgent defenders into accepting a negotiated surrender.[46]

Cruz's Lake Chapala campaign illustrated the complexities of the war and the royalist need to mobilize the society and economy. Many royalist commanders held their posts for lengthy periods during which they developed business interests and engaged in corrupt practices that sapped or deflected their commitment to achieve victory. Throughout the war, livestock stolen by insurgents in Nueva Galicia appeared for sale in the markets of Zacatecas, Guanajuato, León, and other royalist cities. In 1816,

[44]Cruz to Calleja, March 23, 1814, AGN:OG, vol. 149.

[45]Cruz to Calleja, June 10, 1814, AGN:OG, vol. 150.

[46]Cruz to Viceroy Juan Ruíz de Apodaca, Isla Grande de Mezcala, November 25, 1816, AGN:OG, vol. 151. For a detailed discussion of the campaigns surrounding Mezcala see Enrique Cárdenas de la Peña, *Historia marítima de México: Guerra de independencia, 1810–1821* (Mexico: Ediciones Olimpia, 1973), 1:143–174.

Lieutenant Colonel Hermengildo Revuelta,[47] commander of Cruz's division at Lagos, reported that, in two years and four months at this post, he had not been asked once by stock raisers to provide military escorts for herds that crossed insurgent-held territory to provision the cities and towns of the Bajío provinces. Informants who had been with the guerrilla band of Padre Miguel Torres told Revuelta that the level of general trade in the region was not much different under wartime conditions than it had been prior to 1810. Shipments of salt, cotton, and leather goods such as saddles and shoes were dispatched to the *tierra caliente* in exchange for cascalote used in the tanning industry and partially refined sugar.

Witnesses reported widespread commerce in food products, clothing, pelts, muskets, pistols, and swords. Antonio and Marcos Gasca from Valenciana near Guanajuato shipped a chair gilded in silver worth 300 pesos to the rebel chief Pedro Moreno, and it was well known that the insurgents could order anything they wanted from Guanajuato merchants. Indeed, Moreno organized fiesta day markets at Santiago and Comanja, and the rebel leader Rosales held trade fairs at Ibarra where his followers sold mezcal, cotton, salt, and other products to buyers who came from Guanajuato. According to one former rebel, Moreno levied a 15 percent sales tax on these transactions from which he earned 1,000 to 2,000 pesos monthly.[48] Padre Torres shipped flour to supply Guanajuato, and Moreno licensed the campesinos in the region close to León to plant grain under the condition that they pay a tax of 6 pesos per fanega harvested.[49]

Unable to match similar levels of productivity on the royalist side, Revuelta lamented the fact that lands surrounding his fortified garrison at Lagos lay fallow. Despite his efforts to convince the rancheros to cultivate the soil, he was unable to attract any permanent settlers. Given this general situation, he doubted whether the royalists ever could be successful in extirpating the guerrilla bands. Unlike many other district commanders who worked out lucrative arrangements to do business with the enemy, Revuelta was zealous in his campaigns to prevent trade. In 1818, during a predawn

[47]A captain in the Dragones Provinciales de Nueva Galicia, Revuelta was promoted in 1816 to lieutenant colonel and comandante of the Escuadrón de Voluntarios Fieles de Nueva Galicia.

[48]Declaration of Eligio Sedilla, *capitán* and comandante of several companies of Moreno's band, Lagos, February 29, 1816, AGN:OG, vol. 151.

[49]Revuelta to Cruz, Lagos, August 6, 1816; and testimony of Manuel de Reyes, former sergeant in the company of Juan Serna under the command of Pedro Moreno, Lagos, March 21, 1816; and testimony of Casimiro Hernández, corporal in the company of Juan Serna, Lagos, March 25, 1816, AGN:OG, vol. 151. In their testimony, the former rebels mentioned the names of Guanajuato merchants such as Prudencio Nava, José María Alonso, and others who were known only by their first names; many women and youths participated in the trade. One fanega equals about one and one-half bushels.

raid with four hundred cavalry at Tlachiquera in the region of San Juan de Llanos, Revuelta apprehended the insurgent leader Juan Serna, his artillery major Joaquín Estrada, and twelve others. When two of the prisoners confessed that they were merchants from nearby royalist towns, Revuelta executed them on the spot without even the benefit of summary trials.[50]

Of even greater strategic impact than the illegal commerce of the Bajío were the blockade by the Mexican insurgents of the major trade routes to Veracruz and the creation of their own system of licensing and taxing royalist trade.[51] Although powerful royalist columns could force their way through insurgent bands and overrun their fortifications, it was much cheaper for merchants, muleteers, and army commanders to deal with the existing situation. Counterinsurgency operations were expensive and produced only temporary results unless followed up by the establishment of permanent fortified garrisons. In February 1815, for example, Lieutenant Colonel Pedro Zaragoza led a force of the Regimiento Americano and the Dragones de Puebla from Jalapa to Veracruz to convoy a mail shipment. They tore down barriers of felled trees on the roads, filled trenches, destroyed insurgent fortifications at Plan del Río, surveyed recently constructed parapets and other military works at Puente del Rey, and arrived at Antigua to learn that a nearby guerrilla force of three hundred men had closed the road.[52] Zaragosa complained that pursuits of the enemy were made difficult by dense bush, obstacles, and booby traps. Abandoning their light field pieces at the royalist blockhouse, Zaragoza's force assaulted a network of entrenchments. Surprised, the insurgents fled leaving behind some provisions and other supplies. The commander at Antigua informed Zaragoza that no assistance had come from the garrison of Veracruz and that insurgent forces in the district operated without opposition. Continuing toward the coast, Zaragoza's troops exchanged musket fire with two hundred enemy horsemen at Vergara before the insurgents withdrew, leaving bloody trails indicating that some had been wounded. Exhausted by these exertions, the royalist column delivered the mail at Veracruz and departed immediately for Jalapa to encounter new ambushes, rebuilt fortifications, and gunfire from enemy skirmishers who killed several horses and wounded one soldier.[53]

Reviewing Zaragoza's campaign dispatches, Calleja expressed admiration for his operations and confidence that similar pressures elsewhere would diminish insurgent power. At the same time, recognizing that

[50]Revuelta to Cruz, Lagos, February 17, 1818, AGN:OG, vol. 153.

[51]Brigadier José Quevedo, interim governor of Veracruz, to Calleja, May 27, 1815, AGN:OG, vol. 699.

[52]Pedro Zaragoza to Colonel Luis de Aguila, Jalapa, February 14, 1815, AGN:OG, vol. 536.

[53] Ibid.

commerce attracted the Veracruz guerrilla bands, he concluded that all merchant traffic would have to be strictly controlled. Calleja ordered the military comandantes of Jalapa, Córdoba, and Orizaba to embargo all mule trains to and from Veracruz until such times that they could be convoyed by army escorts.[54] As might be expected, this draconian solution was not at all welcomed by the muleteers, traders, merchants, and others who made their living from commerce. They criticized army commanders for exaggerating the *contribuciones* collected in rebel tariffs and doubted their personal motives for supporting the embargo upon unescorted trade between the interior and the coast. At Veracruz, the *consulado* complained that the closures of commerce during 1815 had created a state of "mortal paralysis" in the port city. Instead of following its orders to chase down the insurgents, the army now subjected legitimate commerce to "the empire of bayonets."[55] The Veracruz merchants declared that the army was incompetent in its feeble efforts to extirpate what were in fact small guerrilla bands that interdicted all of the major trade routes to the interior of New Spain.

Despite all efforts by the royalist army, flexible guerrilla tactics and knowledge of the terrain allowed the Veracruz insurgents to survive. In 1816 the royalists failed to sustain their effort to construct a fortified *camino militar* and to situate permanent blockhouses along the main route from the port to Jalapa. Disease, bad climate, desertion, and loss of morale destroyed army units assigned to these duties. Notwithstanding the strong opposition of merchants, Viceroy Juan Ruíz de Apodaca retained Calleja's regulation that mule trains conducting silver, official dispatches, and trade goods must await military convoys. By 1819, however, the Veracruz merchants were almost apoplectic in their insistence that the military end its restrictions and open commerce without escort forces. Noting that a recent counter-insurgency campaign had driven most guerrilla bands away from the major trade routes, they chafed under controls that accomplished little other than to enlist new supporters for Mexican independence. Towns such as Jalapa and Orizaba were cut off from food supplies, manufactures, textiles, and even table salt. Muleteers who conducted pack trains sometimes found that they had to wait for weeks and even months before army convoys escorted them to their destinations. Since many of the smaller operators could not afford to expend their resources during the delays, only the richest merchants and muleteers possessed enough capital to remain in business.[56]

[54]Calleja to Mariscal de Campo José Moreno y Daoiz, March 1, 1815, AGN:OG, vol. 536.
[55]Consulado of Veracruz to the Secretario de Estado y del Despacho Universal de Indias, June 23, 1815, AGN:OG, vol. 216.
[56]Consulado of Veracruz to Apodaca [Venadito], June 9, 1819, AGN:OG, vol. 217.

Although some district army commanders tolerated commerce with insurgents, became rich from contraband trading, and used their authority over convoys to extort fees and bribes,[57] Cruz proposed an aggressive system for Nueva Galicia that was designed to isolate insurgent territories. Beginning in 1813, he prohibited any form of trade with rebel-held regions and warned his commanders that muleteers might also be spies or revolutionary agents.[58] In 1814, Cruz renewed the total ban on commerce and established district patrols to intercept travelers and to verify that they carried valid travel documents. In addition, Cruz denied subjects from royalist zones the right of transit through rebel territory without official military escorts. This order was designed to eliminate contraband trade and also to prevent the insurgents from engaging in the lucrative business of selling travel permits.[59] Confronted with evidence that many merchants and muleteers from Guanajuato travelled the sierras to trade with the insurgents, Cruz criticized the comandante of Guanajuato, Colonel Antonio de Linares, for laxity. In response, Linares argued that while he fully agreed with Cruz's prohibition in principle, his priority was to obtain adequate provisions so that the mining industry could be restored to productivity.[60]

A student of guerrilla warfare and counterinsurgency, Cruz often criticized the approaches of Viceroys Calleja and Apodaca. He suffered no illusions about periodic changes in the tempo of guerrilla activities and held his own views about the real achievements of royalist pacification programs. In January 1815, for example, Cruz rejected Calleja's proclamation that rebel reunions had been reduced to "small gangs of bandits" and that existing royalist units would regain full control of the country. Criticizing the artificial optimism of Calleja's propaganda, Cruz pointed out that the insurrection raged unchecked along the frontiers of the provinces of Guanajuato, Valladolid, and Nueva Galicia where there were neither sufficient troops nor any fortified posts. Cruz informed Calleja, "The whole kingdom knows that large rebel gatherings are taking place and that some others, while not so numerous, are of equal consideration due to the harshness of the terrain where they shelter themselves and for the facility with which they coalesce when it is convenient."[61] Cruz insisted that while he did not mean to belittle the efforts of the viceroy with these hard facts, on a matter of such significance he wanted no one to be deceived. Later, Cruz was equally negative about Viceroy Apodaca's enthusiastic statements lauding the success of pacification and insurgent amnesty programs.

[57]Anastasio Zerecero, *Memorias para la historia de las revoluciones en México* (Mexico: Universidad Nacional Autónoma de México, 1976), 29.
[58]Order of Cruz, November 10, 1813, AGN:OG, vol. 155.
[59]Ibid.
[60]Cruz to Apodaca, December 26, 1815, AGN:OG, vol. 155.
[61]Cruz to Calleja, March 22, 1815, AGN:OG, vol. 161.

Unwavering in his demands for more arms and troops, Cruz's apocalyptic vision contradicted the view of the regime that victory was near. In 1818 when the governor of Zacatecas, Brigadier José de Gayangos, reported a decline in the number of royalist troops to garrison his province, Cruz reminded Apodaca of their conversations during his visit to Mexico City on the nature of the Mexican insurrection. He reiterated to the viceroy his view that existing guerrilla bands in the Guanajuato sierra increased proportionally as royalist units decreased. Without the continuing dedication of competent forces, it would be impossible ever to regain control over the mountainous zones. To achieve success, Cruz stated that royalist soldiers had to live in the mountains for lengthy periods under the same difficult conditions as the insurgents. He argued that it was ridiculous to dispatch royalist columns for fifteen- or twenty-day pursuit operations in the expectation that such efforts would actually produce results.[62]

By 1818, Cruz attributed the royalist failure to achieve total victory to Calleja's 1813 decentralization of military command to the regions, provinces, and districts. In his view, the creation of a network of fortified towns garrisoned by militia forces did not signify the full pacification of a region or province. In Nueva Galicia, Cruz continued to dispatch his mobile divisions against insurgent-dominated districts and to maintain sufficient ongoing military pressure to shift public opinion to the royalists. As a result, the guerrillas had been pressed far back into the mountainous zones along the margins of Guanajuato, Valladolid, and into the *tierra caliente*.[63] Apodaca commended Cruz's approaches but refused to accept the argument that remaining guerrilla bands possessed the powers to coalesce larger forces. Using Zacatecas as an example, he pointed out that the province had been free of significant rebel incursions for two full years. The provincial garrison of 2,327 infantry and 3,248 cavalry, and the proximity of the strong divisions of Colonel Linares and Colonel Francisco de Orrantía, would continue to guarantee royalist domination.

In reality, both Linares and Orrantía would have been shocked by Apodaca's misplaced confidence. The principal weapons of the 364 troops of Orrantía's Cuerpo Provincial de Caballería de la Frontera de Nuevo Santander were lances and machetes. They had muskets captured from the insurgents in previous engagements, but most of these were worn out beyond repair—hardly suitable for chases and skirmishes against guerrilla forces. In April 1818, Orrantía petitioned for replacement carbines, pistols, sabers, and new equipment for his entire unit.[64] Hardly better off, Linares,

---

[62]Cruz to Apodaca, July 10, 1818, AGN:OG, vol. 154.

[63]Cruz to Apodaca, August 14, 1818, AGN:OG, vol. 154.

[64]Subinspector General Pascual de Liñán to Apodaca, April 25, 1818, AGN:OG, vol. 486. In May, Apodaca ordered some replacement weapons sent to Orrantía.

comandante general of the Province of Guanajuato, reported that there were insufficient swords to equip the three dragoon squadrons under his command. When the provincial treasury ran out of funds to pay these troops, some had bartered their swords for food and others deserted with their equipment and uniforms.[65] Apodaca was either poorly informed about the deteriorated state of his garrisons or he believed his own positive propaganda that the war was almost won.

As has been noted, wartime conditions forced army commanders to exercise precedence over the civil administration, and many officers simply usurped all powers within their jurisdictions. The district and regional commanders established *contribuciones militares* to support urban and rural militias, controlled agriculture and stock raising, and regulated communications and commerce through the convoy system. Army officers requisitioned horses for military use and often confiscated mules from civilian transport. Following the reoccupation of insurgent districts, army commanders controlled the distribution of rebel property, held livestock for possible return to legitimate owners, and organized auctions to dispose of unclaimed animals and merchandise.[66] These military administrators received blanket orders to reactivate commerce, restore mining, stimulate agriculture, and assist in special areas such as the shipment of pulque for public consumption in the markets of Mexico City. Army officers controlled police and investigative powers, applied fines and other penalties, and judged and sentenced rebel supporters. They could arrest, punish, and deport anyone and confiscate goods, lands, property, and houses.[67] Many of these powers conflicted with and displaced the jurisdiction of the provincial intendants, district subdelegates, and urban ayuntamientos. As the war progressed, senior officers such as Brigadier Ramón Díaz de Ortega, commander of the Ejército del Sur based at Puebla, favored the complete unification of military, political, and fiscal powers in the hands of the regional comandantes.[68] With the reoccupation of the city of Oaxaca on March 29, 1814, Díaz convinced Calleja to name Brigadier Melchor Alvarez as interim intendant as well as provincial military chief subject to the Puebla command.[69] Ultimately, this concentration of powers designed to end the war permitted army commanders such as Alvarez to acquire wealth and

[65]Apodaca to Linares, June 13, 1818, AGN:OG, vol. 486.

[66]See, for example, Calleja's Instrucción para el comandante general de Llanos de Apan, in Calleja to José Joaquín Marqúes y Donallo, June 18, 1814; and Ramón Gutiérrez del Mazo to Calleja, June 25, 1814, AGN:OG, vol. 530.

[67]Reglamento ó instrucción general para la observancia de los comandantes de partidas patrióticas que han de obrar en la circumferencia de sus respectivos lugares, November 1, 1814, AGN:OG, vol. 430.

[68]Ramón Díaz de Ortega to Calleja, Puebla, no. 666, May 12, 1814, AGN:OG, vol. 529.

[69]Calleja to Díaz de Ortega, May 22, 1814, AGN:OG, vol. 529.

power through fraud, misappropriation of resources, and other forms of corruption.

A European Spaniard, Alvarez had arrived in Mexico in 1813 in command of the expeditionary Batallón de la Infantería de Savoya.[70] Like many European officers, he was haughty, superior, and anticriollo in his attitudes toward Mexicans. In his first posting as *comandante militar* at Jalapa, Alvarez refused to acknowledge the difficulties for the municipal government that had to raise funds to support the urban garrison and also to subsidize the expenses of other military units that passed through the town. Frustrated by the resistance of the local elite, Alvarez requested Viceroy Calleja to appoint "un español verdadero" to head the ayuntamiento or, even better, to terminate debates definitively by subjecting the political sphere totally to the military command.[71]

Despite evident problems with nonmilitary matters and civilians in general, following the expulsion of Morelos, Alvarez became the provincial *comandante militar* and interim intendant of Oaxaca with full administrative, fiscal, and military powers. Given his previous record at Jalapa, it was not at all surprising that he encountered opposition or that he abused his office to make personal profits. Following the reoccupation of Oaxaca, the disposition of insurgent and unclaimed property was a particularly lucrative source of income. Although Alvarez claimed later in his own defense that he had a poor head for figures, it is clear from the documents that he and other officers knew exactly what they were doing. He was charged with misappropriation of funds and theft from the public treasury. Commanders of the army divisions assigned to Oaxaca districts collected and spent tithes, *alcabalas* (excise taxes), tobacco taxes, and even the funds of the Ramo de Bulas (the old Crusade tax).[72] Captain José Antonio Requera, chief of the Sixth Division at Ometepec and Jamiltepec, confiscated raw cotton, distributed it to the women of fifteen villages under his control, and ordered them to produce mantas for his soldiers who were in desperate need of

[70]Hoja de Servicio de Melchor Alvarez, 1815, AGN:OG, vol. 258. Alvarez joined the Spanish army as a cadet in 1786 and achieved the rank of *coronel efectivo* in 1810. He arrived at Veracruz on April 15, 1813, and three days later was in combat at Medellín in command of forces from the Regimientos de Infantería de Savoya and Extremadura. He was related to Mariano de Alvarez, defender of Gerona.

[71]Alvarez to Calleja, Jalapa, July 13, 1813, AGN:OG, vol. 1. When Alvarez arrived at Jalapa, he had funds for only twelve to fifteen days for his expeditionary force. The ayuntamiento stated that in the three years since the war broke out, Jalapa had spent 200,000 pesos to pay its garrison and to subsidize units that passed through the jurisdiction. See Ayuntamiento of Jalapa to Calleja, April 27, 1813, AGN:OG, vol. 32.

[72]Alvarez to Calleja, December 7, 1814, AGN:OG, vol. 1.

clothing.[73] Although Calleja reprimanded Alvarez, the shortage of senior officers in New Spain prevented the viceroy from taking stronger steps.[74] Accustomed to wielding political power and benefiting directly from his offices, in 1821 Alvarez joined many other senior army commanders in support of Iturbide's Plan de Iguala.[75]

Some civilian administrators fought back against the encroachments of military power. The intendant of San Luis Potosí, Manuel de Acevedo, struggled for years to protect his office and the population from the jurisdiction of the commander of the Tenth Militia Brigade, Brigadier Manuel María de Torres Valdivia. The areas of conflict ranged from the abuse of recruitment procedures to numerous questions related to taxation and the funding of army units. Beginning in 1815, Acevedo charged that army recruiters seeking replacements in San Luis Potosí used press gangs, threats, and personal vengeance to round up essential workers. Recruits were held in jail until they were marched off in manacles to join army units as if they were delinquent criminals sentenced to the presidios. Acevedo argued that mistreated recruits often deserted and ended up as insurgents. Even worse, well-to-do families purchased freedom for their young men by bribing the recruiting agents. The intendant asked Viceroy Calleja to remove army officers from recruitment and to invoke the Real Ordenanza de Leva, which placed the corregidores and municipal authorities in charge of levies.[76] In another complaint, the ayuntamiento of San Luis Potosí informed Viceroy Apodaca that it and not the *comandante militar* possessed the legal obligation to propose officer candidates and to recruit soldiers for the Regimientos de Fieles, Dragones de San Luis, Dragones de San Carlos, and the Batallón Ligero de Infantería, which had been raised in the city and its jurisdiction. Torres not only rejected the customary privileges of the ayuntamiento, but he also had proceeded to appoint and promote officers in his command. One of his choices, Ensign Joaquín Basave, a gambler by profession, was infamous for his scandalous life-style with a young woman called Joaquina.[77]

By 1817 the San Luis Potosí provincial dragoon regiments had been absent from their home province for seven years' wartime duty, and in many respects they were difficult to distinguish from the regular line units of the royalist army. As might be expected, after so much time the relatives of

[73]José Antonio Requera to Alvarez, July 15, 1814; and Alvarez to Requera, August 21, 1814, AGN:OG, vol. 1.

[74]Alamán, *Historia de México*, 3:261–262.

[75]Ibid., 5:297.

[76]Manuel de Acevedo to Calleja, San Luis Potosí, August 6, 1815, AGN:OG, vol. 93. Calleja had received complaints from army units that many recruits from San Luis Potosí were incorrigible deserters, gamblers, vagabonds, and criminals. See Calleja to Manuel María de Torres, May 14, 1816, AGN:OG, vol. 93.

[77]Acevedo to Apodaca, April 24, 1817, AGN:OG, vol. 92.

serving militiamen demanded the return of their sons and husbands. Both the mining and agricultural industries, which were the largest employers in the province, resisted new levies to fill vacancies in the regiments, and there were general complaints about the financial burden charged against the treasury of San Luis Potosí.[78] In 1817 the provincial treasury contributed 71,811 pesos monthly to pay the local garrison and those units from the jurisdiction that served elsewhere in New Spain. Added to these expenditures were special costs in 1817 for the pursuit of Javier Mina's invasion force, payment of escorts for the herds of goats and sheep sent to Querétaro for the provisioning of Mexico City, and special expenditures to pay other army units that happened to pass through San Luis Potosí. Despite his best efforts, Intendant Acevedo found that he could not meet all military financial obligations.[79] By 1818 the salaries and allowances of some garrison troops were forty days in arrears and the San Luis Potosí units operating in Guanajuato had not been paid for eight months.[80] Concerned about violence if funds could not be raised to pay the soldiers, Acevedo expressed suspicions that Torres had encouraged his troops to threaten civilian administrators.[81] At San Luis Potosí and other cities of New Spain, eight years of warfare had exhausted available tax revenues. As funding for the war dried up, royalist army commanders had to contemplate other political and military solutions.

Although Acevedo was the chief treasury officer of San Luis Potosí, Brigadier Torres ran his own financial operations separate from the intendancy. Booty captured in combat against the rebels remained under Torres's personal control. In 1815, for example, operations against the insurgent Fernando Rosas resulted in the capture of forty horses, seven muskets, and other property. The intendant received secondhand information about the operation but was not given any detailed inventories. He did learn that two of the best mounts taken from the rebels ended up in Torres's possession.[82] Over the years the level of acrimony between these two officials poisoned relationships and created rival factions in the city. Knowing that Torres rejected any form of cooperation with the civil authorities, Acevedo asked Viceroy Apodaca to settle the matter by transferring one of them out of San Luis Potosí.

[78]Acevedo to Apodaca, May 4, 1817, AGN:OG, vol. 94.

[79]Presupuesto de las cantidades que se deben a las tropas que guarnecen esta capital y otras que operan fuera de ella por alcances del mes de julio, y buenas cuentas respectivas al corriente mes, September 17, 1817, AGN:OG, vol. 94. In 1817 and 1818 the herds of goats and sheep sometimes totalled ten thousand to fifty thousand animals.

[80]Apodaca to Acevedo, May 20, 1818, AGN:OG, vol. 94.

[81]Acevedo to Apodaca, January 7, 1817, AGN:OG. vol. 94.

[82]Acevedo to Calleja, September 6, 1815, AGN:OG, vol. 93.

As might be expected in a war that divided the population, civilians often experienced difficulties in defending themselves against the rapacity and vengeance of army officers. Given the level of polarization caused by the conflict, officers knowingly misconstrued the legitimate rights of individuals as the acts of persons of dubious loyalty or even worse treachery. The commanders of military convoys expropriated food and forage, damaged property, and seldom reimbursed hacendados and villagers. In 1813, for example, Pedro Otero complained that soldiers escorting a silver shipment from Guanajuato, commanded by Iturbide, vandalized his hacienda near Silao. Although Iturbide had orders to requisition hay and straw, his soldiers and muleteers ran amok, smashing Otero's house and the huts of his workers. They chopped up and burned furniture for their cook fires, ripped out a beautiful vineyard, and wrecked the estate's vegetable gardens. Otero approached Iturbide to seek redress and received insulting treatment as if he were "a traitor, a rebel, and a declared and obstinate insurgent." When Otero sent his majordomo to present a statement for damages, Iturbide informed him that "the king pays for nothing."[83]

Otero complained to Viceroy Calleja, stating that he had served the royalist army at the battles of Calderón, Zitácuaro, and in the siege of Cuautla Amilpas. His family had paid millions of pesos over the years in taxes and donations. In the present war, his haciendas suffered losses of over 300,000 pesos caused by insurgent robberies and raids. Even though Otero expressed apprehension about attracting the vindictiveness of Iturbide, he solicited support from the viceroy to achieve redress. In response, Iturbide made no apologies: the furniture in Otero's house was rough and unworthy of consideration; some rooms had no chairs, and wooden chests served as the only seats. If there was no furniture, Iturbide could not see how it could have been broken. Not only did he dismiss what were certainly legitimate claims, but he also did so in a way most damaging to Otero by expressing suspicions that he was a person of dubious loyalty.[84]

In some instances, army commanders behaved like bandits and committed offenses that served to fuel rather than to suppress the insurgency. The adventures of Ignacio Marroquín, renter of the Hacienda de la Concepción near Pátzcuaro, illustrate the point. While Marroquín admitted to having served as an insurgent captain in 1810, he received a full royalist amnesty and returned to a peaceful existence on his lands. Not only did he pay his taxes, but he also contributed two cattle and some sheep each month to the royalist detachment in his district. Although Marroquín had lived as a loyal subject for years, Colonel Felipe Castañon sent a detachment in May 1817 to look for him. Marroquín was absent from his

---

[83]Pedro Otero to Calleja, Guanajuato, August 12, 1813, AGN:OG, vol. 426.
[84]Iturbide to Calleja, Salamanca, October 24, 1813, AGN:OG, vol. 426.

house doing field work when the troops arrived. Unable to locate him, the soldiers condemned him summarily as an insurgent, burned his house and barns, and made off with 7,000 pesos in coin, 780 head of cattle, 1,200 sheep, and 138 pigs.[85] This outrage drove Marroquín into such a fit of anger that he sought out the insurgent leader Padre Torres, who commissioned him as a captain and named him his adjutant. Commanding two hundred insurgent fighters, Marroquín carried out a surprise attack on a convoy from Valladolid. They captured seven dragoons of the Regimiento de Moncada, a sergeant, and eleven *gachupín* civilians. Although Torres ordered Marroquín to execute the prisoners, he released them and even returned some of their possessions.[86] After falling out with Torres about his commitment to insurgency, Marroquín surrendered to the royalists once again and requested a royal amnesty.

Silver miners faced similar arbitrary actions from army officers and often suffered from extortion and other forms of robbery. In 1820, for example, Colonel Cristoval Villaseñor, the *comandante militar* at Majadagrande, a new mining community near Cadereyta, demanded that mine owner Ignacio Lastiri pay 100 pesos monthly rather than the 30 pesos required by law to support the local militias. When Lastiri refused, Villaseñor jailed him until he reconsidered. Merchants paid inflated militia taxes as well and miners received poor treatment from Villaseñor's local administrator, Lieutenant Miguel Ordoñez. For petty offenses this officer sentenced men to fifty lashes, hit others with the flat of his sword, and ordered the miners to congregate their huts at a cramped site where disease and fire were constant dangers.[87]

Although the army commanders often displaced or dominated civilian officials, their political power became more vulnerable over time. Despite the appearance in some regions of a royalist victory in 1816, widespread insurgent activity prevented the recovery of the regional economies. The burden of the *contribuciones militares* fell upon all sectors of the population. In each community, district comandantes organized juntas to seek suitable resources that might be taxed. Generally, the officers nominated subdelegates, local curates, wealthy residents of the headquarters town, and persons from each community of the district. In larger towns and cities the local treasury officer, mining deputy, or representative of the merchant consulado added his expertise and knowledge to the junta. Their

[85]Declaraciones de Ignacio Marroquín, October 12, 1817, AGN:OG, vol. 420.

[86]Ibid. The final break occurred when Marroquín was sent to intercept the mail from Valladolid. Instead of capturing the dispatch riders, he showed himself before the ambush, thus allowing them to take another route.

[87]Representación of the Real Tribunal General de la Minería, Mexico, May 24, 1820, AGN:OG, vol. 511.

task was to raise sufficient funds to support local and regional defenses. In mining regions they established new taxes on silver, retail shops, plaza stalls, and gambling. In farming and stock-raising towns they placed taxes on harvested grain, agricultural products, and on the consumption of luxury goods such as wine. Of even greater concern to the residents, these juntas conducted a detailed census of the entire population of the district to set *contribuciones obligatorias*, which were wealth or income taxes charged to all residents according to their income and total assets. No one was exempt from these taxes, and even the poorest individuals had to pay a real or two from their meager incomes. Hacendados and rancheros paid for militia support according to assessments of the values of their estates, which did not take into account the possibility of insurgent occupations, raids, and interdicted commerce. With wartime taxes a source of chronic discontent, Mexicans looked for ways to terminate a system that they attributed to unnecessarily bloated military expenditures.

As early as 1815 some army commanders began to realize that the Achilles' heel of royalist power was fiscal rather than purely military. Gradually, guerrilla warfare, insurgency, and banditry ground down the tax base and consumed existing sources of Mexican capital. In the Puebla command, Field Marshal José Moreno y Daoiz[88] reported a developing fiscal crisis that threatened the future existence of the royalist army. In January 1815 the Puebla garrison consumed 44,300 pesos for army pay, or about 80 percent of total revenues of 55,059 pesos received by the provincial treasury. Moreno needed another 10,000 pesos to operate his offices before he began to consider other expenditures. Although he attempted to negotiate a loan, even with his best efforts he raised only 4,000 pesos.[89] In the face of growing monthly deficits, most of Moreno's time was taken up in a desperate search for new funds to pay the garrisons of his jurisdiction. Fearful that desertion would erode unpaid units, Moreno and his officers stopped drawing their own pay, and he ordered outlying communities to seek new funds for army pay from local sources.

Despite this instruction, Jalapa requested subsidies from Puebla to pay its garrison, and the fortress of Perote needed at least 3,000 pesos from the Puebla treasury. The army divisions stationed at Orizaba and Córdoba required 15,000 to 16,000 pesos per month from the Puebla treasury since the income from military taxes in those towns barely covered the operating costs of local royalist militias and some operating expenses. Until 1815 royalist commanders had raised 90,000 pesos in the region through

[88]Moreno y Daoiz was transferred to Mexico in 1811 by the regency government. He held many important posts, including subinspector general of the Mexican army until the arrival of Pascual de Liñán, and was *comandante militar* of the Puebla jurisdiction.

[89]Moreno y Daoiz to Calleja, Puebla, January 1, 1815, AGN:OG, vol. 536.

confiscations and forced loans from amnestied rebels, but these sources had been exhausted. Oppressed by the legitimate claims of his subordinate commanders, Moreno begged assistance from the governor of Veracruz, who responded that he had no funds to spare. As a last resort Moreno turned to the central treasury, but Viceroy Calleja dismissed his appeal, noting that all provinces suffered similar financial exigencies. He pointed out that the Mexico City treasury was in even worse shape than that of Puebla. Calleja ordered Moreno to seek his own alternatives and suggested that he require each district commander to impose higher taxes upon reoccupied rebel communities.[90]

Between 1815 and 1820 army commanders could not stave off the financial disasters that gradually eroded the fighting force of the royalist military. It is clear that, even without the emergence of Iturbide, the royalists could not have continued the war for much longer. In September 1820 the *comandante general* of Guanajuato, Colonel Linares, reported that mining production in his province had fallen by 50 percent since 1818. As the recession took hold, the treasuries of agricultural and commercial towns such as Silao and Celaya suffered steep reductions in tax income. Linares reported monthly budget deficits of 15,000 pesos in the fund to pay the Guanajuato army units. Although the Regimiento de Dragones de San Carlos was to have been transferred from Querétaro to Guanajuato, Linares proposed that the move be cancelled since there was no money to pay the troops.[91]

At Querétaro, Brigadier Domingo Luaces wrestled with a monthly army pay deficit of between 11,000 and 12,000 pesos. The viceroy suggested that some mobilized militia companies might have to be disbanded to reduce expenditures, but Luaces rejected this solution since many of these men were amnestied insurgents who would return to their former activities if they were not employed.[92] In the regular units, officers at Querétaro permitted discipline to decline; soldiers without money for daily food robbed market stalls and civilians. In addition, Luaces complained that the arms, uniforms, and other equipment of his troops were in terrible condition and needed replacement. To alleviate the crisis in military funding at Querétaro, he initiated the request to have the Regimiento de San Carlos transferred to Guanajuato and asked that the remainder of the garrison be paid from the general treasury of New Spain. A few months earlier, both Linares and Luaces had made convincing arguments that their provinces needed the assistance of the Regimiento de San Carlos. Now, despite continuing

[90]Calleja to Moreno y Daoiz, January 14, 1815, AGN:OG, vol. 536.

[91]Antonio de Linares to Apodaca [Venadito], Celaya, September 1, 1820, AGN:OG, vol. 460.

[92]Domingo Luaces to Apodaca [Venadito], no. 119, July 17, 1820, AGN:OG, vol. 512.

guerrilla and bandit incursions in both jurisdictions, neither province could afford to pay the provincial dragoons.

On the verge of general bankruptcy, the royalist army needed only one push to topple it into disaster. That act came not from the Mexican insurgents who in 1820 lacked the conventional military power to confront the royalist military on the battlefield, but rather from the Riego Rebellion in Spain and the restored Spanish constitution. After years of subservience, the constitution granted Mexican civilians a weapon to end the dominance of the *comandantes militares*. While some towns swore allegiance to the constitution without ever seeing a copy of the document, others conducted public ceremonies during which orchestras played and the articles were read to the people.[93] In cities and towns throughout the country, the ayuntamientos invoked the constitution to abolish the hated *contribuciones militares*. Following lengthy debates, the municipal authorities terminated militia support taxes and disbanded royalist units that had garrisoned the towns and patrolled the countryside.[94] Although they attempted to fight back, the army commanders could not resist this collapse and the general view in Mexico that the war must end. On October 24, 1820, Viceroy Apodaca published a royal order that prohibited generals, chiefs of division, and other army commanders from collecting taxes in their jurisdictions for the subsistence of the army.[95] In a single blow, the constitution terminated the rule of the royalist army commanders and made it clear that they could no longer maintain the crumbling defense system. While the constitution called for a national militia supported by the central government to replace the decentralized royalist system, few were willing to serve and the ayuntamientos did not enforce the legislation.

Under the constitution, the military temporarily lost the dominance that for years permitted soldiers to control Mexican politics. Some municipal councils went even further to insist that the constitution prevented district army commanders from simultaneously holding the office of *jefe político*.[96] In some communities there were demands for even stronger actions. At Jalapa, the administrator of the royal mail, Faustino de Capetillo, condemned Brigadier Joaquín Castillo y Bustamante, who had governed the town for six years and campaigned against the insurgent Guadalupe Victoria. Capetillo stated that Castillo's "vindictive and vicious" subordinates

[93]José de la Parra to the intendant of Mexico, Ramón Gutiérrez de Mazo, Tixtla, July 4, 1820, AGN:OG, vol. 391.
[94]See, for example, Manuel de Concha to Apodaca [Venadito], Tulancingo, October 31, 1820, AGN:OG, vol. 126; and Ayuntamiento of San Juan del Río to Apodaca [Venadito], July 24, 1820, AGN:OG, vol. 512.
[95]José Dávila to Apodaca [Venadito], Veracruz, November 7, 1820, AGN:OG, vol. 266.
[96]Comandante de San Juan del Río, Gaspar de Reyna to Apodaca [Venadito], December 22, 1820, AGN:OG, vol. 980.

destroyed civil liberties, fomented discord, and abandoned prisoners in the jails. Even after the proclamation of the constitution, Castillo had attempted to continue his dominance over the municipal government and to disregard the law that he had sworn to uphold.[97] Outside of the towns, travelers no longer required passports and army patrols could not tell the difference between royalists and insurgents. Since everyone carried arms, it was almost impossible to separate honest merchants from insurgents, bandits, and army deserters. Men greeted each other with the title of *ciudadano* and often refused to recognize the authority of the military.[98] Perplexed by the rapid pace of change, some commanders confined their troops to barracks.

The suddenness of the collapse of New Spain was remarkable. The proclamation of Iturbide's Plan de Iguala and the simplicity of his message offered soldiers and civilians, royalists and insurgents, an escape from chaos and expectations of a return to prosperity. Although reality would dash these dreams, in 1821 there were no other solutions. Beset by financial crises and the impact of the constitution, the royalist commanders saw the prospect of losing control of their army and their military system. For these officers, Iturbide offered the prospect of commissions and promotions in the Army of the Three Guarantees and the expectation of maintaining the decentralized system of autonomous commands that had served them so well. Few of the Spanish army officers who refused to swear allegiance to the Mexican empire had the stomach for combat against their former comrades. Mexicans who had suffered a decade of debilitating war believed that Iturbide could end insurgency and restore civilian rule. Knowing that they could not win the war on their own, many insurgent leaders accepted Iturbide's compromise. In the momentary euphoria of 1821, the guarantees of religion, independence, and union appeared to end military dominance and regional divisions. In fact, the army commanders were not willing to relinquish their powers and viewed Iturbide as their savior. The struggle for the Mexican nation had just begun.

---

[97]Faustino de Capetillo to José Dávila, Jalapa, July 6, 1820; and Petition of the Ayuntamiento of Jalapa, July 10, 1820, AGN:OG, vol. 266.

[98]Llano to Venadito, no. 1096, November 10, 1820, AGN:OG, vol. 461.

The First Popular Elections in Mexico City, 1812–1813

Virginia Guedea

THE ELECTORAL PROCESSES established by the Constitution of Cádiz during the last years of the colony form a landmark in the political life of New Spain. A new stage, that of direct participation of large sectors of the population, began with those elections. Their significance, however, goes beyond that important fact. On the one hand, by providing new spaces for political participation within the system, the elections also notably affected the process of emancipation because they offered New Spaniards seeking change an alternative to the armed insurrection. On the other, the new forms of political action and organization, which those processes engendered, determined that the electoral model established by the Constitution of 1812 did not end with independence from Spain but continued during the early years of the new nation.

The first popular elections held in Mexico City are significant for various reasons. First, the capital of New Spain was the viceroyalty's most important urban center. Because it was the seat of all authority and the most populous city in the colony, any political activity that occurred there possessed special significance. Second, the manner in which those first elections occurred, as well as their results, determined not only the form of future elections but also their outcome. Finally, this electoral process had

AUTHOR'S NOTE: An earlier Spanish version of this work appeared in *Mexican Studies/Estudios Mexicanos* 7, no. 1 (Winter 1991): 1–28. It is published here with permission from The Regents of the University of California. I thank Jaime E. Rodríguez O. for translating the revised version. I am also grateful to the Rockefeller Foundation for its grant of a residency at Villa Serbelloni, its study and conference center in Bellagio, Italy, which allowed me to work on this essay.

such an impact on the authorities that it occasioned extensive investigations which generated a rich and abundant documentation, thus facilitating research.

A lengthy and complex process, which would have important repercussions in the political life of New Spain and whose influence would be felt after its independence, began when the Junta Suprema Central Gubernativa del Reino (Supreme Central Governing Junta of the Kingdom) decided that it should include not only representatives from the provinces of the Spanish Peninsula but also from its American kingdoms. Largely motivated by the Junta Central's need to obtain American aid and support in order to face the French invaders, the decision would have unforeseen consequences in New Spain. In addition to supporting the claims of many Americans that the viceroyalty was an integral and essential part of the monarchy—a view that the colonial authorities in New Spain had just rejected in a decisive and violent manner—this action renewed the possibility of political participation which had emerged when the Spanish Crown collapsed in 1808, but which seemed foreclosed by the coup d'état of September of that same year.[1]

The Junta Central's decree of January 22, 1809, stated that New Spain, as well as the other viceroyalties and independent captaincies general, should elect a deputy to represent them in that body. The ayuntamientos of the provincial capitals were to play the principal role in holding the election. Each ayuntamiento would elect three individuals "of well known probity, talent, and learning" and choose one of them by drawing lots. From this group, the Real Acuerdo (the audiencia serving as the council of state) and the viceroy, acting as its president, were to select three, from whom the representative to the Junta Central would be elected. The role of the ayuntamientos did not end there. The municipal councils were also to provide credentials and instructions to the deputy elected, a task they addressed immediately since it would assure each of them their own appropriate representation.[2]

The final election, which fell upon Miguel de Lardizábal y Uribe, the representative chosen by the Ayuntamiento of Mexico, would not have major repercussions inside the colony—among other reasons because Lardizábal y Uribe, despite being a native of Tlaxcala, had resided for some

---

[1]See Virginia Guedea, "El golpe de Estado de 1808," *Universidad de México: Revista de la Universidad Nacional Autónoma de México* 488 (September 1991): 21–24.

[2]Lucas Alamán, *Historia de Méjico desde los primeros movimientos que prepararon su independencia en el año de 1808 hasta la época presente*, 5 vols. (Mexico: Imprenta de J. M. Lara, 1849–1852), 1:291–292; José Miranda, *Las ideas y las instituciones políticas mexicanas: Primera parte, 1521–1820*, 2d ed. (Mexico: Instituto de Investigaciones Jurídicas, UNAM, 1978), 226–227.

time in the Peninsula and apparently did not represent any particular group within the viceroyalty. Nonetheless, the electoral process, restricted though it was, provides some interesting insights about the colony. Among those nominated were many who enjoyed great prestige and power in New Spain. Furthermore, the majority—eight of fourteen—had been born in the Peninsula, and they were closely aligned with its interests since they occupied important civil, military, and ecclesiastic posts in New Spain and had distinguished themselves, or would distinguish themselves, as ardent defenders of the colonial system and the status quo. Unquestionably, they were representatives of what may be called imperial interests, and their election makes manifest the prestige that individuals of that class and status possessed in some regions of the viceroyalty at that time. Among those selected were the military men Félix María Calleja, by San Luis Potosí, and Bernardo Bonavía, by Durango; Bishop Juan Cruz Ruiz de Cabañas, by Guadalajara; and the judge of the Audiencia of Mexico, Guillermo de Aguirre, by Querétaro. Nevertheless, although in the minority, individuals who either questioned or would later question the system, such as Bishop Manuel Abad y Queipo and the *cura* of the Burgo de San Cosme, José María de Cos, were also elected, by Valladolid and Zacatecas respectively. Their election suggests that certain reformist and even autonomist tendencies, as well as interests that might be called domestic, also found expression in that process.[3] As a consequence of the elections, the ayuntamientos of New Spain began to regain the role which some of them, especially the Ayuntamiento of Mexico, so strenuously had sought in 1808: that those corporations possess the fundamental right to represent the provinces of the realm, a crucial factor given the critical circumstances of the Spanish monarchy at that time.

When it convened a cortes, the Regency, which succeeded the Junta Central and included Lardizábal y Uribe as one of its five members, provided new opportunities to the ayuntamientos. In its decree of February 14, 1810, the Regency declared that the Spanish dominions in America and in Asia should "participate in the national representation of the special cortes," which already had been convoked in the Peninsula. This time, each province was allocated a deputy who would be elected by the ayuntamiento of every provincial capital. As had occurred in the elections for the Junta Central, each ayuntamiento would select three individuals "endowed with probity, talent, and learning and without any blemish," from whom a representative was to be chosen by drawing lots. As in 1809 the deputies were to receive

---

[3]"Relación circunstanciada de los sujetos electos por las provincias del Virreynato para el sorteo de Diputado de la Suprema Junta Central," in Archivo General de la Nación (hereafter AGN), Historia, vol. 418, f. 1–3.

instructions from their ayuntamientos. However, in contrast to the previous election, the deputies had to be natives of the provinces they represented.[4]

That requirement, reinforced by the Regency's proclamation accompanying the decree—in which it not only reiterated that the dominions of America and Asia were integral parts of the monarchy, and therefore possessed the same rights as the Peninsula, but also declared that from that moment the American Spaniards had been elevated to the category of free men[5] —affected the outcome of the elections. The increasing discontent of New Spaniards with a regime that refused to recognize their desire to participate in the decision-making process also influenced the elections. In contrast to the experience of 1809, many of those who participated in the *ternas* (ternary), as well as most of those finally elected deputies, were individuals whose interests were clearly linked to those of their localities and who sought greater autonomy at the viceregal as well as at the provincial level. There were many clergymen elected, such as doctors José Miguel Guridi y Alcocer, *cura* of Tacubaya, for Tlaxcala; José Miguel Ramos Arizpe, *cura* of the Real de Borbón, for Coahuila; Antonio Joaquín Pérez, canon of Puebla, and José Miguel Gordoa, professor of the Seminary of Guadalajara, for Puebla and Guadalajara respectively. In addition, Dr. José Ignacio Beye de Cisneros, canon of Guadalupe, a declared autonomist and a friend and defender of deposed Viceroy José de Iturrigaray, was elected for Mexico. They all played an active and brilliant role in the cortes, defending the equality of representation between America and Spain and advocating provincial autonomy.[6]

The elections for deputies in many other parts of the Spanish empire, including the Peninsula, resulted in outcomes similar to that of New Spain. The special cortes was dominated by the *liberales*,[7] individuals who were determined to transform and modernize the political system of the empire. Their efforts culminated in 1812 in the Political Constitution of the Spanish Monarchy, which was promulgated in Cádiz on March 19, 1812, and proclaimed in the capital of New Spain on September 30 of that year. The charter, which created a unitary state with equal laws for all the Spanish

---

[4]J. Miranda, *Las ideas y las instituciones*, 229–230; Alamán, *Historia de Méjico*, 1:334–335.

[5]Alamán, *Historia de Méjico*, 1:217.

[6]Ibid., 1:appendix, 50; Charles R. Berry, "The Election of Mexican Deputies to the Spanish Cortes, 1810–1822," in *Mexico and the Spanish Cortes, 1810–1822*, ed. Nettie Lee Benson (Austin: University of Texas Press, 1966), 16.

[7]The term *liberal* was coined for the first time in the Cortes of Cádiz. The two principal groups in that congress were known as the *liberales* and the *serviles*.

dominions,[8] could not have been implemented at a worse time for the colonial regime in New Spain. The highest colonial authorities, the viceroy and the audiencia, who for two years had been facing an armed insurgency that appeared to gain greater vigor as it was becoming more widespread, saw their power reduced by a cortes, which desired to impose greater administrative control on the part of the metropolis, at a time when discontent grew daily among those who wanted a greater role, within the system, in the decision-making process. And if that were not enough, the implementation of the constitution offered new opportunities for political participation to a large group of New Spaniards because the charter abolished old privileges, declaring all Spaniards equal before the law.[9] Those actions would strengthen those who were discontented with the system.

The colonial regime in New Spain, therefore, refused to implement in full the constitution. Nevertheless, the authorities were forced to accept its fundamental dispositions and to proceed to reorganize the viceroyalty at three levels: local, provincial, and imperial. The process of change was to begin with the creation of constitutional ayuntamientos and provincial deputations, as well as with the selection of the deputies who would represent New Spain in the next regular cortes, which would convene in October 1813. All this required extensive electoral processes in which those who enjoyed the rights of citizenship—that is, large sectors of the population—would participate as voters. Furthermore, the ayuntamientos were to play an important role in those processes.

The electoral procedures established by the cortes were not only indirect but also lengthy and complex. There were two stages for elections to the constitutional ayuntamientos: the selection of parish electors; and the designation of the new alcaldes, *regidores* (councilmen), and syndics by the electors. The election of deputies to the cortes and to the provincial deputations was even more intricate. Elections to these two bodies occurred at three levels: parish, *partido* (district), and province. Because of their complexity, preparatory juntas were necessary to organize and conduct them.

The viceroyalty was divided into five regions for the elections of deputies to the cortes: New Spain itself, New Galicia, Yucatán, the Eastern Interior Provinces, and the Western Interior Provinces. One more province

---

[8]Jaime E. Rodríguez O., "From Royal Subject to Republican Citizen: The Role of the Autonomists in the Independence of Mexico," in *The Independence of Mexico and the Creation of the New Nation*, ed. Jaime E. Rodríguez O. (Los Angeles: UCLA Latin American Center Publications, 1989), 34.

[9]The Constitution of 1812 abolished the distinctions between the two republics—the one for Spaniards and the other for Indians. All men were declared political citizens, except the blacks and *castas*. On this point consult James F. King, "The Colored Castes and the American Representation in the Cortes of Cádiz," *Hispanic American Historical Review* 33 (February 1953): 33–64.

was added for the elections of provincial deputations: San Luis Potosí, to which was joined Guanajuato.[10] The Preparatory Junta for New Spain, consisting of the provinces of Mexico, Puebla, Michoacán, Oaxaca, Veracruz, Tlaxcala, Querétaro, Guanajuato, and San Luis Potosí—these last two only for the elections of deputies for the cortes—met in Mexico City at the end of October 1812. In accordance with the requirements of the cortes, the Preparatory Junta consisted of Viceroy Francisco Xavier Venegas, as *jefe político superior*; Canon José Mariano Beristáin, named by the *cabildo eclesiástico sede vacante* (cathedral chapter with the archbishop absent);[11] Ramón Gutiérrez del Mazo, intendant corregidor of Mexico; Juan Cervantes y Padilla, the senior *alcalde ordinario*; José Antonio Méndez Prieto, *regidor decano* (senior councilman); José María Fagoaga, *alcalde del crimen* (magistrate of the criminal chamber); and two *vecinos buenos* (good neighbors), the Mariscal de Castilla and Marqués de Ciria and the Conde de Bassoco. Through the 1792 census, the Preparatory Junta determined that the region of New Spain would elect forty-one deputies, with fourteen of those, plus four substitutes, corresponding to the Province of Mexico. It also stipulated that the provincial deputation of the region of New Spain would consist of seven members. In addition, it determined that elections would take place in the *ciudades cabezas* (capital cities) of the *partidos* which were free of insurgent control, and it set February 1, 1813, as the date when the *partido* electors were to congregate in the capital.[12]

The date selected by the Preparatory Junta passed without the final elections being held. Because of events that took place at the beginning of a less complex and strictly local electoral process—that of the constitutional ayuntamiento of Mexico City—the higher authorities suspended, at least temporarily, both the capital's municipal elections as well as the elections for deputies to the cortes and to the provincial deputation.

The Constitutional Ayuntamiento

The ayuntamiento then in office, by and large, conducted the first popular elections held in Mexico City. That body established the number of electors to be chosen by each parish, determined the number of juntas or

---

[10]Royal Decree and Instructions of the Cortes, May 23, 1812, published in Mexico on October 10, 1812, in AGN, Historia, vol. 447, cuad. 1, f. 8; "Parecer de los fiscales," Mexico, September 27, 1812, in ibid., vol. 447, cuad. 1, f. 6–7v.

[11]Whenever the archbishop or the bishop was absent, the *cabildo eclesiástico* operated as a *sede vacante* (vacant see).

[12]Proclamation of Intendant Ramón Gutiérrez del Mazo, Mexico, November 27, 1812, AGN, Historia, vol. 445.

sessions to be held in each of them, and designated members of the cabildo who would supervise the vote. Those decisions, the requirements which those designated as electors had to meet, and the date of the election, Sunday, November 29, 1812, were announced in a proclamation of the intendant corregidor and *jefe político*, Gutiérrez del Mazo.[13]

Despite the care taken by the election organizers, who included Viceroy Venegas, they failed to define such clearly important aspects as the qualifications of those eligible to vote or the site where *vecinos* of a parish with more than one junta were to vote. The capital also lacked an electoral register, which resulted in considerable confusion, doubt, and much unease. Furthermore, the elections aroused great interest among many *capitalinos* (residents of the capital), who celebrated the event with noisy and tumultuous acts, reactions which concerned the regime. But it was the election results themselves which, more than anything else, convinced the authorities virtually to suspend the entire electoral process. All those selected as the city's twenty-five electors were American born, some were disaffected with the system, others were known insurgent sympathizers, and none was a partisan of the regime. Under the pretext of avoiding in future elections the problems that had emerged in these, the authorities initiated investigations and inquiries that were essentially motivated by their need to discover why events had occurred as they had and who was responsible for them.

The documentation generated by this first stage of the electoral process, and particularly as a consequence of the unease of the regime, is very rich and allows us not only to determine precisely what happened but also to analyze carefully many of its facets. In the first place, we can determine how each of the capital's seventeen parish juntas conducted the elections. We can also discover the attitude assumed by the various members of the ayuntamiento entrusted with presiding over those meetings. Further, the documentation permits us to learn how different groups conducted pre-electoral activities. In addition, it provides a clear view of the behavior of the city's population both during and after the elections. Finally, it allows us to understand the repercussions of the electoral process on the political life of the capital.

Because the Constitution of 1812 did not grant political citizenship to blacks and *castas* and suspended the voting rights of debtors, domestic servants, the unemployed, and those under criminal indictment, determining who possessed the franchise presented a serious problem for the officials of the juntas. The charter, however, permitted the parochial electoral juntas to

---

[13]Proclamation of Intendant Ramón Gutiérrez del Mazo for elections to the Ayuntamiento, Mexico, November 27, 1812, in *La Constitución de 1812 en la Nueva España*, 2 vols., ed. Rafael Alba (Mexico: Secretaría de Relaciones Exteriores, Imprenta Guerrero Hnos., 1912–1913), 1:226–230.

resolve doubts in these matters.[14] Although the constitution excluded large sectors of the capital's population from voting, several parish electoral juntas did not enforce those restrictions. The reports indicate that in some cases the junta presidents, either on their own or in consultations with the *vecinos* present, actually restricted the suffrage. Others, however, permitted indiscriminate voting, without taking into account *pelaje* (appearance) or "color," as junta presidents themselves indicated. There were also instances of individuals either voting or intending to vote more than once, a fact that worried some officials. That problem was particularly evident in El Sagrario parish, which possessed four electoral juntas.

The elections made manifest certain political and social realities. On the one hand, certain sectors of the capital's population were rootless and lacked stability, mainly as a result of the war of insurgency that the viceroyalty then experienced. On the other, they highlighted something much more important: during this first stage of the electoral process, in which many individuals voted who did not have that right according to the constitution, we can see that the population of the capital had begun to outgrow the divisions into which society had been organized, compartments in which ethnic distinctions played an important role. That is, the old model—the caste society—was no longer corresponding to reality.

Electoral junta officials also had to resolve, at their discretion, another question. Many voters arrived at the polling places carrying *papeletas* (slips of paper) with the names of their candidates written on them, and many of these were the same size and written in the same hand. In addition, many of those who carried these slips did not know the names on them, and many voice votes coincided exactly with the written ones. These factors led the authorities, not without reason, to talk about a "conspiracy."[15]

It is evident, from the elections themselves as well as from their results, that many people must have engaged in well-coordinated pre-

[14]Articles 22 and 50 of the Constitución Política de la Monarquía Española, in Juan E. Hernández y Dávalos, *Colección de documentos para la historia de la guerra de independencia de México de 1808 a 1821*, 6 vols. (Mexico: Biblioteca de "El Sistema Postal de la República Mexicana," José María Sandoval, 1877–1882), 4:88, 90.

[15]Antonio Annino, who in an interesting work has made a careful and in-depth analysis of the elections of November 29, 1812, finds that the distribution of these *papeletas* varies in relation to the ethnic composition and the location of the parishes. It was more intense in those where the population was very mixed and fluctuating. He also finds a relationship between the way the *papeletas* were handed out and the results of the elections. Some lawyers were elected where more *papeletas* were distributed and where fluctuating population was greatest, in contrast to other parishes where primarily clergymen as well as former Indian governors were elected. See Antonio Annino, "Pratiche creole e liberalismo nella crisi dello spazio urbano coloniale: Il 29 novembre 1812 a Città del Messico," *Quaderni Storici* (69) 23, no. 3 (December 1988): 727–763.

electoral activities. In its "Representación" to the cortes of November 1813, the Audiencia of Mexico indicated the existence of a "conspiracy," citing a list containing the names of those who would later be elected which had been circulated throughout the city days before the election. Such a list does not prove the existence of a cabal, but it does indicate that there had been a selection of candidates. Furthermore, during the elections, porters had been paid to distribute the *papeletas* with the names of the candidates selected.[16] While I have been unable to determine who, in particular, participated in these activities, we know that a clandestine group of *capitalinos* called the Guadalupes, who aided the insurgent movement in various ways, took part in these pre-electoral activities. Although there is no mention of that group, nor of its activities, in the documentation of the election, shortly thereafter the Guadalupes sent a letter to the insurgent leader José María Morelos in which they refer to their participation in the electoral process.[17]

I have located evidence of the participation in the elections of one of those identified as a member of the Guadalupes, the Canon Dr. José María Alcalá, a well-known insurgent sympathizer who on various occasions had openly expressed his discontent with the colonial regime. Alcalá was accused not only of directing the elections and of holding meetings in his house to influence the results but also of having declared "that he would prefer to see himself in jail rather than allow any European to be named *regidor*."[18] Another member of the Guadalupes, the municipal councilman Joaquín Caballero de los Olivos, also took part in the pre-election activities. He, however, acted in an open and public manner as the member of the capital's cabildo charged with presiding over the electoral junta of the parish of San José. Finally, another Guadalupe, Fagoaga, the Mexico City *regidor* and *alcalde del crimen*, who presided over the parish junta of El Salto del Agua, also participated in the pre-election organization.

The electoral success of the Americans has obscured another important fact: the autonomists and malcontents were not the only ones who engaged

---

[16]"Representación de la Audiencia de México a las Cortes," Mexico, November 18, 1813, in Emilio del Castillo Negrete, *México en el siglo XIX, o sea su historia desde 1800 hasta la época presente*, 19 vols. (Mexico: Imprenta del "Universal," 1881), 7:appendix, 373–374.

[17]Letter from "Los Guadalupes" to José María Morelos, Mexico, December 7, 1812, in *Los Guadalupes y la Independencia, con una selección de documentos inéditos*, ed. Ernesto de la Torre Villar (Mexico: Editorial Porrúa, 1985), 9.

[18]Carlos María de Bustamante, *Martirologio de algunos de los primeros insurgentes por la libertad e independencia de la América mexicana* (Mexico: Impreso por J. M. Lara, 1841), 9–10; Alamán, *Historia de Méjico*, 4:38; Alejandro Villaseñor y Villaseñor, *Biografías de los héroes y caudillos de la independencia: Con retratos*, 2 vols. (Mexico: Imprenta de "El Tiempo" de Victoriano Argüeros, 1910), 2:120.

in pre-electoral activities. The Europeans and other partisans of the colonial regime also organized themselves for the elections. There were, therefore, two clearly defined parties, or groups, in open opposition: the Americans and the Europeans. Lucas Alamán indicates that both groups distributed extensive lists with the names of their candidates in the days before the election.[19] As Intendant Gutiérrez del Mazo, who presided over one of the electoral juntas of El Sagrario parish, declared in his report: "There were 496 [votes] in writing in favor of Dr. Alcalá and Villaurrutia, Dr. Torres, and Licenciado [López] Matoso, and 99 for D. Luis Madrid, D. Gabriel Yermo, D. Tomás Terán, and D. Francisco Cortina"; subsequently he corrected the figures, indicating that there had been 521 for the first group and 75 for the second.[20] The intendant also discussed the oral ballots in his report, indicating that people voted verbally "in favor of one or the other party," a statement that demonstrates both the existence, and the recognition by the authorities, of the two parties as well as the fact that they carried out pre-electoral activities. The figures provided by Gutiérrez del Mazo also demonstrate that in the most "Spanish" of parishes, where the greatest number of European Spaniards resided, the Americans triumphed over them by a ratio of almost seven to one.

The members of the ayuntamiento who presided over the juntas did not agree completely about the elections. Eleven of the seventeen presidents of the parish juntas, among them Caballero de los Olivos and Fagoaga, declared in their reports that they had not experienced problems regarding either voter qualifications or multiple voting. Thus, the majority of the members of the old ayuntamiento fully endorsed the electoral process. The others also approved it, demonstrating more or less reserve, depending on the circumstances. The difference in attitudes found among the members of the capital's cabildo also occurred among the electors. Although all the electors were Americans, and none a partisan of the colonial regime, their attitudes ranged from open and determined sympathy for the armed insurgency or the persistent questioning of the legitimacy of the colonial authorities to the most respectful observance of the guidelines established by those officials. But, irrespective of these differences, like the ayuntamiento, the majority of the electors—if not all of them—had a common goal: to obtain significant political changes within the system and, particularly, to ensure that Americans would take charge of the city's government. United around that common interest, they formed alliances and joined forces.

[19] Alamán, *Historia de Méjico*, 3:289.
[20] "Informe del intendente Ramón Gutiérrez del Mazo," Mexico, December 19, 1812, in AGN, Historia, vol. 447, cuad. 1, f. 62–64, published in Alba, *Constitución de 1812*, 1:239–241; Oficio of Intendant Ramón Gutiérrez del Mazo to Viceroy Francisco Xavier Venegas, Mexico, January 11, 1813, in AGN, Historia, vol. 447, cuad. 2, exp. 10, f. 3–5.

There were various members of the society of the Guadalupes among the electors: Alcalá himself and *licenciado* Antonio Ignacio López Matoso, both for the parish of El Sagrario; *licenciado* Pedro Dionisio de Cárdenas for Santa Cruz; and the Indian former governor of the *parcialidad* (Indian community) of San Juan, Dionisio Cano y Moctezuma, for Santo Tomás la Palma. Electors closely allied with the society included: the *alcalde de corte* Jacobo de Villaurrutia for El Sagrario; *bachiller* José Manuel Sartorio and *licenciado* Carlos María de Bustamante for San Miguel; the military man Francisco de Arroyave for Santa Catarina, and another Indian former governor of San Juan, Francisco Antonio Galicia, for the parish of Acatlán. Juan de Dios Martínez, an elector for Santa Catarina, was also involved with the insurgents since he was related by marriage to the insurgent leader Julián de Villagrán, with whom he was in correspondence.[21] Their names are mentioned here because several of them would later take part in other electoral processes where they would exercise notable influence.

The differences in postures of greater or lesser radicalization among the electors reflect, to a great extent, the different interests that came together in those elections. There is little doubt that the electoral exercise awakened the interest of the great majority of the people of the capital for a variety of reasons. Leaving aside the minority of Europeans, almost all of them partisans of the status quo and therefore determined to support the colonial authorities, it is evident that for the rest of the population the elections of November 1812 provided opportunities that could not be lost. For the autonomists, they opened a new and extensive legal means to immediately achieve their aspirations for home rule. The electoral process permitted the city's ayuntamiento to once again become their spokesman, as it had been in 1808, and thus to regain, strengthened, its traditional political legitimacy vis-à-vis the colonial authorities. For partisans of the insurgency, the elections represented a splendid opportunity to weaken the colonial regime and to link the insurgent movement with the interests of the autonomists. And for the Indians of the capital's two *parcialidades*, in particular for their officials, they provided the only possibility of obtaining political representation since, according to the constitution, the Indian communities were to disappear and with them their special form of government. Thus, all groups united in support of a common cause: that the control of all the urban space fall into their hands.

Besides the important interests that were at stake, the unusual nature of the situation, which allowed popular meetings to be held where all—or almost all—the city's inhabitants could openly express their opinion about who should elect those persons who would be charged with the government

---

[21]"Electores para el Ayuntamiento de México," Mexico, December 2, 1812, in Hernández y Dávalos, *Colección de documentos*, 4:675–676.

of the capital, provoked a festive spirit in many sectors of the population. The gathering held in the *casas consistoriales* (city halls) to reach the final vote count, a meeting attended by a large public, as well as the final results, increased the merrymaking, which lasted until the following day. Masses of people roamed throughout the city, even during the night, with cries of "Long live the electors, America, the nation, and the Virgin of Guadalupe!" There were also shouts for the criollos, the Americans, the editors of the newspapers *El Juguetillo* and *El Pensador Mexicano*—Bustamante and José Joaquín Fernández de Lizardi—as well as the insurgents Ignacio Allende and Morelos. There were some who shouted for Joseph Bonaparte and those who exclaimed that the people were sovereign. Some even called for death to the *gachupines* and to Fernando VII himself. There were also massive demonstrations of support for the electors, in particular for Alcalá, Villaurrutia, Sartorio, and Bustamante.[22] Despite the authorities' opposition, the supporters rang the bells of the cathedral and other churches. Finally, a group appeared in front of the viceregal palace demanding that they be given cannon for artillery salvos, which was not allowed.

Fearing that such popular enthusiasm would get out of control, the authorities kept the troops in their barracks, and on the afternoon of Monday, November 30, the intendant ordered everyone to retire to their houses.[23] The people obeyed. The regime's concern was not due solely to the popular demonstrations of joy that the elections elicited; it was also the result of denunciations of supposed plans to overthrow the viceroy and eliminate the Europeans,[24] as well as rumors that the people of the surrounding towns had been convened to the capital to celebrate the elections, and reports of the joy that the election results had given to the insurgents.[25] But the concern was also the product of more serious questions.

The authorities' real problem was that the colonial regime found itself in an exceptionally critical situation. On the one hand, the armed insurrection taking place in various parts of the viceroyalty had won a

[22]See Declaration of José María Galán, Mexico, February 11, 1813, in Alba, *Constitución de 1812*, 2:252–253; declaration of José Miguel Gutiérrez, Mexico, February 4, 1813, in ibid., 2:253–254; declaration of Manuel Villaverde, Mexico, February 12, 1813, in ibid., 2:254–255; declaration of Rafael Pérez, Mexico, February 12, 1813, in ibid., 2:256–257.

[23]Alamán, *Historia de Méjico*, 4: 290–291.

[24]Declaration of José María Falces, Mexico, December 6, 1812, in AGN, Historia, vol. 447, f. 19–19v; declaration of Juan de Dios Núñez, Mexico, December 6, 1812, in ibid., vol. 447, f. 20; Francisco Rodrigo to Viceroy Francisco Xavier Venegas, December 4, 1812, in ibid., vol. 447, f. 23.

[25]José Yáñez to Jacobo de Villaurrutia, Mexico, December 9, 1812, in ibid., vol. 447, f. 41; Certification of Julián Roldán, Mexico, December 11, 1812, in ibid., vol. 447, f. 49.

number of important victories, such as Morelos's capture of Oaxaca a few days before the elections were held in Mexico City. On the other, the popular elections had provided not only the autonomists, those disaffected with the regime, and the partisans of the insurgency but also the formerly tranquil Indians of the city's *parcialidades* with the opportunity to find common interests and to unite their efforts to achieve their ends through very diverse and effective means of communication. The elections had demonstrated that a group was forming which aspired to autonomy and which enjoyed the support of large sectors of the population. This group, with the cabildo as a base, possessed the capacity to direct and mobilize the city. Control of the urban space was now in their hands, not in those of the colonial authorities.

And if that were not enough, the recently decreed freedom of the press had given rise to open and public questioning of the system. Convinced of the "dismal and terrible change in the public spirit caused by freedom of the press," the viceroy and the audiencia decided to suspend it.[26] They also ordered confiscated all the publications that appeared at that time as well as the detention of the two writers most famous for newspapers that seriously questioned the colonial system: Fernández de Lizardi and Bustamante of *El Pensador Mexicano* and *El Juguetillo*. One of them, Bustamante, who had also been chosen elector, fled the city. Finally, the authorities proceeded against other electors, such as Villaurrutia, whom they forced to leave the capital, and Martínez, whom they detained and charged with corresponding with his in-law, the insurgent Villagrán.

With ongoing investigations about the elections and with the imprisonment, exile, and flight of three of the electors, the electoral process was de facto suspended, even though both the old ayuntamiento as well as the new electors insisted that the process be concluded.[27] That would not

[26]Real Acuerdo of December 5, 1812, in Hernández y Dávalos, *Colección de documentos*, 6:455.

[27]José María Alcalá, José Manuel Sartorio, José Julio García de Torres, Juan de Dios Alanís, José García de Villalobos, José Mariano de Lecca, Marcos de Cárdenas, Dionisio Cano y Moctezuma, Mariano Orellana, Luciano Castorena, Juan de Dios Martínez, Francisco de Arroyave, José Blas de las Fuentes, José Norzagaray, Francisco Antonio Galicia, Conde de Xala, Antonio Ignacio López Matoso, José de Ferradas, José Antonio de Mendoza, Pedro Dionisio de Cárdenas, and Manuel Victoria Tejo to Ramón Gutiérrez del Mazo, Mexico, December 27, 1812, in Alba, *Constitución de 1812*, 1:244–245; the Ayuntamiento of Mexico to Viceroy Francisco Xavier Venegas, Mexico, December 29, 1812, in Hernández y Dávalos, *Colección de documentos*, 4:839–840; José María Alcalá, Ignacio María Sánchez Hidalgo, José Julio García de Torres, Antonio Ignacio López Matoso, José de Ferradas, Manuel Victoria Tejo, José García de Villalobos, José Blas de las Fuentes, Luciano Castorena, Juan de Dios Alanís, Marcos de Cárdenas, Pedro Dionisio de Cárdenas, José Mariano de Lecca, Conde de Xala, José María Torres, Mariano Orellana, José Antonio de

occur until four months after the first stage had been conducted. The process was renewed, not because the investigations determined whether or not the elections had been valid but because Calleja, the new viceroy, decided to implement the constitution, insofar as possible, in hopes of attracting to the regime the sympathies of those who were partisans of the constitutional system.

With the elector Martínez freed and Villaurrutia permitted to return to the capital, the authorities established April 4, 1813, as the day for the selection of the alcaldes, *regidores*, and syndics of the constitutional ayuntamiento of Mexico City.[28] Although I have been unable to locate the documentation generated by this election, we know from Alamán that Calleja pressured the electors and had the archbishop exhort those who were clergymen, in order to have some Europeans chosen. It was to no avail; once again, only Americans won.[29] In a letter to Morelos, the Guadalupes noted that other persons, without explaining who they were, also tried to influence the elections. They indicated that "there had been weak electors who allowed themselves to be seduced by Calleja's agents; [but] God, who watches over us, granted strength to the plurality and the votes came out as we desired since there is not a single *gachupín* in the ayuntamiento."[30] The Guadalupes certainly had reason to maintain that they had achieved the desired results: three of them were elected *regidores*. The documentation of this election also refers to the important and decisive participation of Canon Alcalá, much as he had done in the first stage of the process. His electoral activities, his sympathy for the insurgency, and his hostility to the colonial regime—particularly the decree against clerical immunity—caused the archbishop to initiate proceedings against him.[31]

The Guadalupe-elected *regidores* were: Francisco Manuel Sánchez de Tagle, a landowner and former *regidor* of the capital's old ayuntamiento; Ignacio Adalid, a landowner and *letrado* (legal scholar); and Ignacio Moreno, the Marqués de Valleameno. Galicia, the Indian former governor who was closely involved with the Guadalupes, was also elected *regidor*,[32] as was

---

Mendoza, and José Manuel Sartorio to Ramón Gutiérrez del Mazo, Mexico, December 3, 1813, in Alba, *Constitución de 1812*, 1:244–246.

[28]"Aviso al público," April 3, 1813, in AGN, Historia, vol. 447, cuad. 2, f. 30.

[29]Alamán, *Historia de Méjico*, 3:412.

[30]Letter of "Los Guadalupes" to José María Morelos, Mexico, December 9, 1812, in Torre Villar, *Los Guadalupes*, 24–25.

[31]Villaseñor y Villaseñor, *Biografías*, 2:120; Bustamante, *Martirologio*, 9–10.

[32]On the role of the leaders of the Indian *parcialidades* of Mexico City see Virginia Guedea, "De la fidelidad a la infidencia: Los gobernadores de la parcialidad de San Juan," in *Patterns of Contention in Mexican History*, ed. Jaime E. Rodríguez O. (Wilmington, DE: Scholarly Resources, 1992), 95–123.

José María Prieto Bonilla, a relative of one of the Guadalupes, and Caballero de los Olivos, a former *regidor*. The Conde de Medina y Torres, a colonel and landowner, who was suspected by the authorities of being an accomplice in the conspiracy against Viceroy Venegas in April 1811,[33] was elected alcalde. The other alcalde selected was Antonio de Velasco y Torre, a merchant and landowner who was a friend of Leona Vicario, one of the women working with the Guadalupes, as well as of Bustamante's wife.

The election would have important consequences. An ayuntamiento constituted entirely of Americans, many of them hostile to the regime, would once again become the voice of those in the capital who sought autonomy. While the institution regained its traditional political legitimacy vis-à-vis the colonial authorities, given the attitude of its members it would inevitably become the opponent of the regime. Since both contenders as well as those who supported them joined battle without quarter, their respective positions became even more polarized.

The Deputies to the Cortes and to the Provincial Deputation

Despite the results of the election for the constitutional Ayuntamiento of Mexico City—results unfavorable to the colonial regime—the viceroy continued in his determination that the elections ordered by the constitution be carried out in the capital of New Spain. Therefore, he established Sunday, July 4, 1813, as the date of the first phase of the complex process that would culminate in the designation of deputies to the cortes and to the provincial deputation. By then several of the *partidos*, which together with Mexico City were to participate in those elections, had already initiated the process of naming electors.

The authorities took various measures to prevent the repetition of the events of November 1812. On the one hand, in January 1813 they requested that the *curas* of the capital inform the authorities of the number of the faithful in each parish. In the following April they notified the public that the constitutional ayuntamiento would form a detailed and accurate census of each parish as soon as possible in order to obtain a precise count of the faithful to determine the number of electors allotted to each parish.[34] On the

---

[33]See Virginia Guedea, "The Conspiracies of 1811: Or How the Criollos Learned to Organize in Secret," Paper presented at the conference on The Mexican Wars of Independence, the Empire, and the Early Republic held at the University of Calgary on April 4–5, 1991.

[34]Viceroy Francisco Xavier Venegas to parish *curas*, Mexico, January 9, 1813, and their replies, in AGN, Historia, vol. 447, exp. 10; Notice of Intendant Ramón Gutiérrez del Mazo, Mexico, April 23, 1813, in Alba, *Constitución de 1812*, 1:166.

other hand, they held a *junta preparatoria* to organize the elections. The extensive decree that convened the capital's citizens to attend parish electoral juntas explained in detail how many sessions each parish was to hold, who were the members of the ayuntamiento, or in one instance the intendant corregidor who would preside over them, and the location of the meetings. It also indicated that the respective parish *curas*, or their deputies or vicars, were to attend, and that a secretary and two scrutineers were to be named for each session. The decree further established the number of electors that each junta would name; these would be selected by thirty-one *compromisarios* (arbiters) chosen by the *vecinos* of each parish. In addition, the decree specified the days on which the juntas were to be held because, in contrast to the provisions for the elections of November 1812, different days were established for different parishes. Although not explicit, the intent was to control the electoral process and to avoid, insofar as possible, any occasion for popular demonstrations.[35] Finally, the decree established Sunday, July 11, as the date when electors for the capital's *partido* would be designated. Then they, together with the other *partido* electors from the Province of Mexico, would elect the deputies to the cortes on Sunday, July 18.[36]

From the little that I have been able to learn about the election of the capital's parish electors—since virtually no contemporary author refers to it and the documentation that I have located so far is very scarce—it appears that the authorities obtained their objectives only in part. There were neither disturbances nor popular demonstrations of enthusiasm. This was probably the result of the dispositions of the authorities. But I believe that the terrible and very deadly epidemic that the city suffered at the time also affected public reaction.[37] According to Alamán, while there was no unrest on that occasion, there was confusion and disorder regarding who was eligible to vote. He further indicates that the juntas accepted all *papeletas* presented with the names of the *compromisarios*. That practice, it should be noted, was neither irregular nor illegal. The decree itself indicated that the voters

---

[35]According to the proclamation, the electoral junta of the Sagrario parish would be held on Sunday, July 4, and would be divided into eighteen sessions. On Monday the 5th would be held those of San Miguel, Santa Veracruz, San José, and Santa Catarina Mártir parishes, each divided into four sessions, except the last which would have six. The other parishes would hold theirs on Wednesday the 7th: Soledad de Santa Cruz, San Sebastián, and San Pablo, divided into three sessions; Santa Ana, Salto del Agua, and Santo Tomás la Palma with two sessions each; and Santa María, Santa Cruz Acatlán, and San Antonio de las Huertas, which would only hold one session per parish.

[36]Proclamation of Intendant Ramón Gutiérrez del Mazo, Mexico, July 2, 1813, in AGN, Historia, vol. 445.

[37]The nature of the epidemic is not clear. Some physicians referred to "pestilential fevers," others to "the fevers of 1813." Apparently, several diseases were involved. See Donald B. Cooper, *Epidemic Disease in Mexico City, 1761–1813* (Austin: University of Texas Press, 1965), 157–182.

might carry lists of their candidates. That provision appears entirely reasonable since one had to vote for thirty-one individuals. Finally, Alamán indicates that the results were the same as those of November 1812: all those elected were Americans.[38]

The lists that I have been able to locate for this election—those for *compromisarios* for the parishes of El Sagrario and San José, and for electors for the parishes of San Miguel, Santa Veracruz, and El Salto del Agua—demonstrate that Alamán was correct insofar as those chosen were Americans. The names of well-known autonomists appear in those lists, such as *licenciados* Juan Nazario Peimbert y Hernández, a member of the Guadalupes who was elected *compromisario*, and Ricardo Pérez Gallardo, Juan Bautista Raz y Guzmán, Antonio Ignacio López Matoso, and José María Jáuregui, all of them chosen electors and all members of the society of the Guadalupes. Another Guadalupe, Lieutenant José María Alba, was selected *compromisario*. Also listed are members of the old ayuntamiento, such as *licenciado* Agustín Villanueva Cáceres de Ovando, elected *compromisario*, and the elector Manuel Gamboa. In addition, some of those chosen electors in November 1812 were also selected this time, such as López Matoso, doctors Ignacio María Sánchez Hidalgo and José María Torres Torija, *licenciados* Luciano Castorena and José Antonio de Mendoza, and Mariano Orellana. The lists, however, also include a former judge of the Audiencia of Mexico, José Arias de Villafañe, who was chosen *compromisario* as well as elector.[39] As occurred in the elections for the ayuntamiento, diverse interests managed to come together in this one; that also would be reflected in its results.

The minutes of the *junta electoral de partido* of July 11 indicate that *licenciado* López Matoso was named secretary and *licenciado* Raz y Guzmán and Francisco Cendoya scrutineers; the latter were charged with examining and approving the credentials of the parish electors. The minutes also show that "a great number of citizens" attended, and that 155 of the 158 electors were present. They selected as *partido* electors Dr. Alcalá and Sánchez de Tagle, the first by a vote of 151 and the second by 144 votes.[40] But as interesting as the results of the voting were "two accidents," also recorded in the minutes, that occurred when the entire junta marched under its standards to the cathedral to attend the required Te Deum. One resulted from the

[38]Alamán, *Historia de Méjico*, 2:423.

[39]"Lista de los compromisarios de la parroquia del Sagrario," AGN, Historia, vol. 448, f. 127; "Lista de los compromisarios de la parroquia de San José," AGN, Ayuntamientos, vol. 168; "Lista de los electores de las parroquias del Sagrario, San Miguel, Santa Veracruz, San José y Salto del Agua," AGN, Ayuntamientos, vol. 168.

[40]"Acta de la junta electoral de partido," Mexico, July 11, 1813, in AGN, Ayuntamientos, vol. 193, f. 3–7v.

unwillingness of the president of the *cabildo eclesiástico*, Dr. Beristáin, to permit the tolling of bells to celebrate such an important event, a refusal that forced the members of the junta first to stand waiting on foot in the middle of the street and later to return to the *casas consistoriales*. The other incident occurred during that disagreeable delay, when the viceroy and his escort left the palace; with all deliberateness and without any consideration their carriages passed through the middle of the procession, cutting it in half. Both incidents, occurring to "a body as respectable as a gathering of the electors representatives of all the Mexican people,"[41] wounded their sensibilities and provoked their protest. Although the much-desired tolling of bells was finally achieved and the Te Deum celebrated with the greatest of solemnities, and although the junta itself excused the viceroy, the occurrences of July 11 make manifest two important factors: the increasing displeasure with which the viceregal authorities viewed the elections, and the decision of those who made up the electoral junta to validate their rights and to insist upon the recognition they deserved.

The installation of the junta of *partido* electors on July 16 was carried out with a little more than one-half of the electors present—twenty-seven of the forty-two who should have been there, to which two were later added—since insurgents occupied eight of the *partidos* and seven others had not held elections. Sánchez de Tagle was elected secretary of that body and Alcalá and José Miguel Guridi y Alcocer scrutineers, charged with reviewing and approving the credentials of the electors of the junta. The analysis of the officials, recorded in the minutes, indicates that the electoral process had presented varying degrees of difficulty in different *partidos* and in some instances lent itself to irregularities because specific requirements were not met. Nonetheless, all the credentials presented were approved and their defects overlooked because of the "scarcity of electors" and in order not to offend any of those present.[42] Alamán makes an important comment regarding the practice; he noted that it would establish a precedent that would have repercussions in the political life of independent Mexico, since that "vicious practice" would also be followed in future congresses.[43] The minutes of the *junta electoral* record another significant fact: since that session the few electors on the European side—only five—began to manifest their opposition to the way the electoral process was handled. When Guridi y Alcocer suggested that the *foráneos* (out-of-town) electors propose, on their own, individuals from their respective *partidos* with

---

[41]The term "Mexican" is used here to refer to the people of Mexico City. At that time the region was known as the Viceroyalty of New Spain; it is only after Independence that the country takes the name Mexico.

[42]"Acta de la junta electoral de provincia," Mexico, July 16, 1813, AGN, Historia, vol. 448, exp. VI, f. 98–102.

[43]Alamán, *Historia de Méjico*, 3:423.

whom to form a list, Juan Madrid y Quiñones, elector from Texcoco, argued in vain against the practice, stating that such lists were contrary to the constitution.[44]

As the minutes of the July 18 session to select deputies for the cortes demonstrate, the European electors continued their opposition from the start of that meeting. The elector Madrid read a paper in which he declared the junta null for lack of sufficient electors, an objection that did not win approval and that was supported by only one other elector, Manuel Ascorve, also a European and also from Texcoco. But in spite of the opposition of the European Spaniards, the results of the vote were the same as in previous elections. Not a single European was elected deputy to the cortes.

The nature of the voting highlights the two tendencies that emerged in the junta: the strength of each side, and who were their candidates. In every instance, the Americans obtained from eighteen to twenty-three votes, the Europeans from three to nine. Among the candidates of the latter group were such staunch supporters of the colonial system as *licenciado* Juan Martín de Juanmartiñena, the *fiscal* (Crown attorney) Francisco Xavier Borbón, the inquisitor Bernardo del Prado y Obejero, and Madrid himself. The majority, however, consisted of nobles, some of whom were not known to be unconditional supporters of the regime. In addition, we find the Indian former governor, Cano y Moctezuma, an elector in 1812 and a member of the society of the Guadalupes, who may have been selected because the Europeans insisted upon including an Indian among the deputies. The fourteen proprietary deputies and four substitutes elected, all of them supported by the Americans, included eleven lawyers, six clergymen, and only one landowner, the Marqués del Apartado.[45] Alamán notes another precedent here; he indicates that "since that election clergymen and lawyers have almost exclusively dominated the congresses, where the productive classes have always had too little place."[46] A final observation about the deputies: although two of these lawyers were members of the constitutional ayuntamiento—Dr. Tomás Salgado and *licenciado* José Antonio López Salazar—and two others were Guadalupes—*licenciados* Félix Lope de Vergara and Manuel Cortázar—there were among those representatives the same diversity of positions as occurred in November 1812 and in the first stage of the electoral process of 1813. That was also true among the Europeans themselves.

On the day following the election of deputies for the cortes, the *partido* electors proceeded, as the constitution required, to designate the deputies for

[44]"Acta de la junta electoral de provincia," Mexico, July 16, 1813, AGN, Historia, vol. 448, exp. VI, f. 98–102.

[45]"Acta de la sesión de la junta de electores," July 18, 1813, in ibid., vol. 448, exp. VI, f. 103–115.

[46]Alamán, *Historia de Méjico*, 3: 423.

the Province of Mexico who would constitute part of the provincial deputation. Since the Province of Oaxaca was then occupied by the insurgents, Mexico would elect two deputies, plus a substitute. The ratio of votes on this occasion was the same as on the previous day, and the results remained the same. According to the Guadalupes,

> this was where they [the Europeans] received the greatest blow since elected were [Guridi y] Alcocer, a former deputy to the cortes, and don José María Fagoaga, European by birth but raised and educated in this kingdom; he is a great partisan [of the American cause], a man of liberal ideas, and an *hombre de bien* [a man of high social standing]. That was the greatest blow to our enemies because, for them, Fagoaga is worse than the most insurgent of Americans. Licenciado Cristo, born in Havana and an excellent subject for the post, was elected substitute deputy.[47]

The Guadalupes were correct. Guridi y Alcocer, who, as indicated earlier, had been elected deputy to the cortes in 1810, had distinguished himself in that body as a champion of equal rights for all Spaniards and for proportional representation in the cortes for all Spanish dominions. He also gained distinction as one of the principal architects of those organs of local autonomy, the provincial deputations. Fagoaga, who had been a member of the Preparatory Junta for these elections and who had presided over the parish junta of El Salto del Agua in November 1812, was a member of the Guadalupes. Finally, *licenciado* José Antonio del Cristo y Conde, besides being a member of the Guadalupes, was a well-known autonomist since the events of 1808.

The European electors were naturally dissatisfied with the results of the election and they impugned them in the junta itself. As the minutes indicate, elector Madrid challenged Guridi y Alcocer's designation as a member of the provincial deputation on the grounds that he was a clergyman and that he had served as a deputy to the cortes. After Guridi y Alcocer replied to these objections, both left the session so that the issue could be freely discussed. As he left, Madrid exclaimed "that this had no other remedy than to eliminate all the criollos with cannonfire," a statement immediately reported to the junta by a member of the "people" who asked that the "people" receive the appropriate satisfaction. The session ended with Madrid's denial that he had used such a phrase, a conciliatory attitude among those who managed the meeting, and shouts by the public in attendance of "Long live those elected!"[48]

---

[47]Letter of "Los Guadalupes" to José María Morelos, Mexico, August 5, 1813, in Torre Villar, *Los Guadalupes*, 46.

[48]"Acta de la sesión de la junta de electores," July 19, 1813, AGN, Historia, vol. 448, cuad. 16, exp. V, f. 3–6v.

Matters did not end there, however. Several European electors, besides refusing to sign the minutes of the sessions or retracting their signatures, later lodged protests with the viceroy. Although he hindered the electoral process in accepting their objections and in ordering an investigation of the case, he also occasioned the gathering of extensive documentation that allows us to learn how the last stage of the elections developed. Just as the materials generated by the concerns of the authorities with the occurrences of the elections of November 1812 allow us to learn in detail how the first stage of the electoral process, that of popular participation, took place, the documentation gathered about the events of 1813 offers us the opportunity to see how the later phase, that of the junta of *partido* electors, developed.

Three European electors protested in writing against the election proceedings: Madrid and Ascorve, who have already been mentioned, as well as *bachiller* José Antonio Pol y España, elector for Tacuba. The three insistently alleged that a plot had been formed among the American electors to arrange through "bribery or contrivance" to exclude completely the Europeans and to ensure that certain candidates, all of them Americans, were elected. To achieve those ends, the American electors had held pre-election meetings at night in the house of Canon Alcalá, whom the Europeans accused of being petulant and haughty, as well as the *corifeo* (leader) of the elections. In those meetings the Americans had elaborated lists, which were later distributed, of those whom they wanted to win—a victory they in fact achieved. Finally, the European electors complained that they had been the object of ridicule of the people who attended those elections and who celebrated the triumph of the Americans with shouts of "Long live the victors!" In order to provide support for their arguments, to win the goodwill of the viceroy, and to provoke the displeasure of the winning party as well as to alleviate their feelings of frustration and even resentment, the three made a number of significant observations. Madrid and Ascorve asserted that the election of deputies to the cortes had been yet "another warning given in Mexico [City] to those in authority of the abhorrence that [the Americans] have for Spain, its government, and all us Spaniards who live here."[49] Pol y España went even further in telling the viceroy that no one doubted "that attempting to win all [public] offices via the constitution and taking arms against the government was one and the same thing, or at least a secret alliance." And he ended by declaring that also one could not doubt that when the very sons of the European Spaniards "unite with Indians, blacks, and the *canalla* [rabble] to destroy and to kill us, simply for having been born in Spain," it becomes necessary "to use force to repel their insolence, handling it with the degree of justice required by the most cruel,

---

[49]Juan Madrid y Quiñones and Manuel Ascorve to Viceroy Félix María Calleja, Mexico, August 7, 1813, in ibid., vol. 448, exp. VI, f. 80–80v.

most barbarous, most extraordinary persecution that ever appeared upon the Earth."[50]

The Americans, particularly those who had been in charge of the elections, responded immediately and forcefully. The principal supervisors of the electoral process—Alcalá, Guridi y Alcocer, Sánchez de Tagle, and the intendant corregidor himself, Gutiérrez del Mazo—replied with appropriate politeness to all the imputations point by point. The Americans firmly denied that the intent of their actions had been the total exclusion of Europeans; the election of the European-born Fagoaga clearly demonstrated the falsity of that allegation. But, they argued, even if the American electors had desired that their deputies also be American, the Europeans were not being offended simply because the Americans wished to be represented by their countrymen, inasmuch "as it is natural to suppose that they would be more devoted to their country and generally more likely to know it better" than the Europeans. Therefore, they had acted from completely understandable and natural feelings and not out of hatred for the Europeans, as Madrid and Ascorve maintained. But even supposing that there had been hostility toward European Spaniards, that enmity was not enough to infer that there was also hatred toward Spain or its government. There had also been no reason to claim, as had Pol y España, that an attempt to use the constitution to win all public offices was the same as taking up arms against the regime. That statement, they maintained, was either disrespectful of the constitution or extravagant nonsense.[51]

The Americans, however, did not deny having discussed the candidates and having agreed upon who should be elected. On the contrary, they considered such action appropriate. Alcalá made it clear that not to have organized would have indicated a serious lack of responsibility on their part and more than likely would have led to criticisms from the Europeans, since then they would have had "further reason to call us automatons, unsociable, and rustics." Thus, he openly acknowledged the meetings which different groups of electors held at different locations, one of which had been Villaurrutia's house, as well as having elaborated various lists of candidates, which they then compared and corrected so that later they could vote for whomever they considered best.[52] The Europeans themselves had conducted similar activities. According to López Salazar, in a statement confirmed by several witnesses, Pol y España had visited him to request his help in being

---

[50]José Antonio Pol y España to Viceroy Félix María Calleja, Mexico, July 26, 1813, in ibid., vol. 448, exp. VI, f. 74–75.

[51]Ramón Gutiérrez del Mazo, José Miguel Guridi y Alcocer, Francisco Manuel Sánchez de Tagle, and José María Alcalá to Viceroy Félix María Calleja, Mexico, January 14, 1814, in ibid., vol. 448, exp. VI, f. 176–177.

[52]José María Alcalá to Viceroy Félix María Calleja, Mexico, January 17, 1814, in ibid., vol. 448, exp. VI, f. 134–135.

elected deputy to the cortes, promising all those who would vote for him that he then would vote as they desired. While discussing the question, Pol y España had shown him a list of candidates which, he said, he had received from the archbishopric.[53]

In his very long and very interesting written statement, Alcalá attempted to dispel the charges that he had been the leader of the American electoral campaign. He indicated that, both in the elections for the constitutional ayuntamiento and for deputies, he had always been the first among the electors, "with such a large number of votes that one can almost say that I was elected by acclamation." His election was not the result of his seeking votes, he averred, but because he merited the "universal regard" of El Sagrario parish, having been earlier its *cura* and now the canon prebend. He also acknowledged that the majority of electors voted for him but pointed out that this also was not the result of his efforts. On the contrary, various electors had sought him out in order to learn his opinion; the archbishop himself had sent the Conde de Jala to visit him in order to reach an understanding about the elections.[54] Although the canon, in all honesty, declared in his written statement that he would not attempt to dispel the charges of being petulant and haughty, it is evident that nothing was further from his mind. It is also clear that despite his protests to have done nothing to achieve it, he was, without doubt, the central figure in those elections and that he enjoyed enormous influence. Both his attitude and his activities explain why the authorities initiated secret proceedings against him at the end of 1813 in order to learn the extent of his actions and his influence on those elections. As already indicated, the archbishop had also initiated proceedings earlier for similar reasons.[55]

The documentation of the elections reveals the presence of an important participant, who would become one of the principal actors during the entire phase of this process and who was the subject of much comment by members of both parties: "the people."[56] The determined support that the people gave to the Americans, and the rejection and ridicule to which they subjected the Europeans, and which so distressed them, allowed the former to argue, correctly in my opinion, that the actions of the people fully confirmed the results of the electoral process. As Intendant Gutiérrez del Mazo indicated, if the people considered the exclusion of the Europeans from

[53]José Antonio López Salazar to Viceroy Félix María Calleja, Mexico, October 30, 1813, in ibid., vol. 448, exp VI, f. 134–135.

[54]José María Alcalá to Viceroy Félix María Calleja, Mexico, January 17, 1814, in ibid., vol. 448, exp. VI, f. 187–191v.

[55]"Causa reservada, 1813," in AGN, Infidencias, vol. 76, n. 4.

[56]See Virginia Guedea, "El pueblo de México y las elecciones de 1812," in *La ciudad de México en la primera mitad del siglo XIX*, 2 vols., ed. Regina Hernández Franyuti (Mexico: Instituto de Investigaciones Dr. José María Luis Mora, 1994), 2:125–165.

public office in the elections their victory, one could not speak of an accord or plot by a few "since it was according to their [the people's] intention and desire." On the contrary, the general will had been fulfilled.[57]

It is obvious that regardless of how large a public attended these events, it could not have included all the city's inhabitants, but only a certain number of them. Who, then, were the "people" so often referred to in these proceedings? The intendant's report clarifies in part that question. He declared that those who attended the session were not the *canalla* mentioned with disdain by the Europeans. Among the "citizens" present, he recognized "many of the first rank, and nearly all the others from the middle class of the estate."[58] We may add that the actions of these citizens suggest that, in their majority, they must have been Americans. After all, they were the ones who had the most to gain from the elections. Through the electoral process they could take part in decision making and see their interests represented at the highest level of government—in the cortes—and at the provincial and local levels in New Spain, both in the provincial deputations and in the municipalities.

The documents also demonstrate that the election brought into the open the struggle between Europeans and Americans. It was a conflict clearly acknowledged in the many charges of the former and the many replies of the latter. During this struggle, both sides defined their positions and goals more precisely and clearly. Here it is worthwhile defining the use of the terms "American" and "European" found in the documents, which this essay follows. While these words never lost their original meaning, regarding place of birth, they acquired a heavy political content. They came more and more to refer to a strong attitude either of support for or of opposition to the colonial regime in New Spain. These views were held primarily, but not exclusively, by those born on this or that side of the Atlantic. They were based, more than anything else, on the orientation of their interests: either toward the Peninsula or the interior of New Spain.

Finally, the European electors were not the only ones to question the elections. Several *vecinos* from Oaxaca, among them two *curas*, complained to Viceroy Calleja about the designation of Fagoaga as their representative to the provincial deputation. They requested that someone born in Oaxaca, residing in Mexico City, be appointed to that office.[59] Although the Electoral Junta successfully argued that Fagoaga had not been elected explicitly as a deputy from the Province of Oaxaca but that the Province of

---

[57]Ramón Gutiérrez del Mazo to Viceroy Félix María Calleja, Mexico, December 16, 1813, in AGN, Historia, vol. 448, exp. VI, f. 147-147v.

[58]Ibid.

[59]José María Prejamo y Capitán, Joaquín de Urquijo, Jerónimo de la Riva, Juan Nepomuceno Binuet, and Juan Antonio Munita to Viceroy Félix María Calleja, Mexico, July 21, 1813, in ibid., vol. 448, exp. V, f. 21–24v.

Mexico had named two representatives because Oaxaca was occupied by the insurgents, Fagoaga immediately realized the significance of the problem. He wrote the viceroy that the complaint of the Oaxacans was not directed at him personally. Rather, "it was intended to vindicate the rights of the Province of Oaxaca which have been slighted because none of the many individuals born there or *vecinos* of that province, then residing in Mexico City and who possessed all the qualifications to hold that office with distinction, have been chosen."[60] This incident is of great significance, even if it refers to only one case, because it represents a phenomenon that would become increasingly important in the political life of New Spain and later in independent Mexico: the demands of the provinces vis-à-vis the center. The electoral processes reinforced autonomist tendencies both at the viceregal and local levels. These demands would find not only an outlet for their expression in the politics of elections but also a means to achieve satisfaction.

Of the individuals selected in the three elections examined in this essay, only the members of the capital's constitutional ayuntamiento and one deputy to the cortes would carry out the duties to which they were elected. The provincial deputation of New Spain would not be installed until a year later, and then as a result of a new election. With the exception of Cortázar, the deputies to the cortes were unable to travel to the Peninsula because the colonial authorities refused to provide them the funds necessary to get there. These obstructions did not disenchant the people of the capital. They continued to join forces and to form alliances to take full advantage of the elections that occurred during the constitutional period from 1812 to 1814, and subsequently when the constitution was restored in 1820.

Regardless of their results, as time went on the electoral processes would attract increasing interest and obtain greater participation at all levels. This occurred, above all, because elections would become the principal channels of expression for the different interest groups in New Spain while offering new opportunities for political organization and action within the system. As a result of the electoral process, the politics of New Spain not only expanded but also achieved a new dynamic.

---

[60]José María Fagoaga to Viceroy Félix María Calleja, Mexico, August 7, 1813, in ibid., vol. 448, exp. V, f. 25–26v.

The Constitution of 1824 and the Formation of the Mexican State

Jaime E. Rodríguez O.

Q. What is the Spanish Nation?
A. The union of all Spaniards of both hemispheres.
Q. Who are Spaniards?
A. According to the Constitution [of 1812], Spaniards are: 1) all free men born and residing in Spanish dominions and their children; 2) foreigners who have obtained citizenship papers; 3) those who, without them [citizenship papers], legally reside ten years in any town of the monarchy; and 4) freedmen who acquire their freedom in the Spanish dominions.
Q. Is the king not sovereign?
A. The king is a citizen, just like everyone else, who obtains his authority from the nation.
Q. What are the rights [of Spaniards]?
A. Liberty, security, property, and equality.
Q. Could these rights be abused or abrogated?
A. Spaniards regained their rights after despotism had usurped them. The heroic efforts they made and are making to maintain their independence are convincing proof that they will not permit anyone to despoil them of their liberty, which is assured by the exact observance of the wise Constitution they have sworn [to uphold].

Catecismo político (1820)[1]

THE CONSTITUTION OF 1824, independent Mexico's first charter, represented the culmination of over a decade and one-half of profound political change. It reflected the experience of a generation of New Spaniards who, while

AUTHOR'S NOTE: An earlier Spanish version of this essay appeared in *Historia Mexicana* 40, no. 3 (January–March 1991): 507–535. It is published here with permission from that journal. I am grateful to the Rockefeller Foundation for an

initially seeking home rule, ultimately opted for independence as the only way to rule at home. In the process, the people of New Spain ceased being subjects of the Crown and became citizens of Mexico. That transformation was evolutionary, not revolutionary. The government of the new Mexican nation evolved naturally from the traditions and institutions of New Spain. Independence did not constitute, as is often said, the rejection of the colonial heritage and the imposition of alien ideas and structures.

Beginning in the 1780s, the Viceroyalty of New Spain experienced debilitating changes. The expansion of commercial agriculture transformed the most prosperous regions of the kingdom, driving campesinos into marginal areas or off the land. In addition, a series of agricultural crises resulted in food shortages, famine, and death. After a period of prosperity, mining and textile manufacturing also entered an era of decline. Increased competition from Europe further damaged internal production. These economic reverses coincided with political changes that adversely affected New Spaniards. The Bourbon reforms restricted or eliminated the ability of the American Spaniards, the criollos, to participate in local government.[2] As a result of the wars unleashed by the French Revolution, the Spanish Crown raised taxes, confiscated Church wealth, and imposed forced loans.

---

opportunity to expand and revise this work at Villa Serbelloni, its study and conference center in Bellagio, Italy. Research for this article was made possible by a grant from the University of California, Irvine, Academic Senate Committee on Research, the University of California President's Fellowship in the Humanities, and a Fulbright Research Fellowship. I also thank Linda A. Rodríguez, William F. Sater, and Virginia Guedea for suggestions for improving this essay.

[1]D. J. C., *Catecismo político arreglado a la Constitución de la Monarquía Española; para la ilustración del Pueblo, instrucción de la juventud, y uso de las escuelas de primeras letras* (Puebla: Imprenta San Felipe Neri, 1820).

[2]There is extensive literature on the late eighteenth-century transformation. See: Enrique Florescano, *Precios del maíz y crisis agrícolas en México, 1708–1810* (Mexico: El Colegio de México, 1969), 85–197; idem, *Origen y desarrollo de los problemas agrarios en México, 1500–1821* (Mexico: Editorial Era, 1976), 71–131; David Brading, *Miners and Merchants in Bourbon Mexico* (Cambridge, England: Cambridge University Press, 1971); idem, *Haciendas and Ranchos in the Mexican Bajío: León, 1700–1860* (Cambridge, England: Cambridge University Press, 1978); Eric Van Young, *Hacienda and Market in Eighteenth-Century Mexico: The Rural Economy of the Guadalajara Region, 1675–1820* (Berkeley: University of California Press, 1981), 192–269, 273–342; Claude Morin, *Michoacán en la Nueva España del siglo XVIII* (Mexico: Fondo de Cultura Económica, 1979); John Tutino, *From Insurrection to Revolution in Mexico: Social Bases of Agrarian Violence, 1750–1940* (Princeton: Princeton University Press, 1986), 61–90; John Super, "Querétaro Obrajes: Industry and Society in Provincial Mexico," *Hispanic American Historical Review* 56, no. 2 (May 1976): 197–216; and Richard J. Salvucci, *Textiles and Capitalism in Mexico: An Economic History of the Obrajes, 1539–1840* (Princeton: Princeton University Press, 1987), esp. 157–166.

Because of these increasing exactions, the financial structure of the colony disintegrated; and, as John TePaske has demonstrated, "the financial collapse of . . . [New Spain] was almost an accomplished fact by . . . 1810."[3]

Although these crises severely strained the viceroyalty, New Spaniards remained loyal to the monarchy. It was the imperial crisis of 1808, the collapse of the Spanish Crown and the imprisonment of the monarch by the French, however, that triggered the process of political change in New Spain. Faced with an emergency of unprecedented proportions, colonial Mexicans proposed the formation of a regional cortes, a parliament of cities, to resolve the constitutional crisis created by the political vacuum in the Peninsula. The European Spaniards rejected the pretensions of the criollos, overthrew the viceroy, and seized the government. Thereafter, conflict ensued between American Spaniards, who desired home rule, and the European Spaniards, the *peninsulares*, who insisted that the colonial relationship be maintained.[4]

Events in Spain had profound effects in the New World. Unwilling to accept French domination, Spaniards organized provincial juntas to oppose the invader. Although initially divided, the provinces of Spain ultimately joined forces to form a government of national defense, the Junta Suprema Central, and to wage a war of liberation. The Spanish national government, however, could not defeat the French without the aid of the colonies. Therefore, the new regime recognized the equality of the American kingdoms and in 1809 invited them to elect representatives to the Junta Central.[5]

[3]John Jay TePaske, "The Financial Disintegration of the Royal Government of Mexico during the Epoch of Independence," in *The Independence of Mexico and the Creation of the New Nation*, ed. Jaime E. Rodríguez O. (Los Angeles: UCLA Latin American Center Publications, 1989), 63. See also Romeo Flores Caballero, *La contrarrevolución en la independencia* (Mexico: El Colegio de México, 1969), 28–65. See also my comparison of New Spain with France in Jaime E. Rodríguez O., "Two Revolutions: France 1789 and Mexico 1810," *The Americas* 47, no. 2 (October 1990): 161–176.

[4]The principal work on the 1808 crisis is Virginia Guedea, "Criollos y peninsulares en 1808: Dos puntos de vista sobre lo español" (Licenciatura thesis, Universidad Iberoamericana, 1964); and idem, "El golpe de Estado de 1808," *Universidad de México: Revista de la Universidad Nacional Autónoma de México* 488 (September 1991): 21–24. See also José Miranda, *Las ideas y las instituciones políticas mexicanas*, 2d ed. (Mexico: Universidad Nacional Autónoma de México, 1978), 235–254; Luis Villoro, *El proceso ideológico de la revolución de la independencia*, 3d ed. (Mexico: Universidad Nacional Autónoma de México, 1981), 41–69; Jaime E. Rodríguez O., "From Royal Subject to Republican Citizen: The Role of the Autonomists in the Independence of Mexico," in Rodríguez, *The Independence of Mexico*, 22–30; and Guadalupe Nava Oteo, *Cabildos de la Nueva España en 1808* (Mexico: Secretaría de Educación Pública, 1973).

[5]Virginia Guedea, "Las primeras elecciones populares en la ciudad de México, 1812–1813," *Mexican Studies/Estudios Mexicanos* 7, no. 1 (Winter

Although limited to a small urban elite, the elections enhanced the political role of the municipalities, the ayuntamientos. They were the first in a series of elections that provided New Spaniards with the opportunity to participate in government at various levels. In 1810 the Spanish government convened a cortes, inviting the American kingdoms to send delegates. The elections to the cortes extended the franchise more broadly than those for the Junta Suprema Central, thus offering colonial Mexicans greater opportunities for political participation.[6]

The Spanish Constitution of 1812 increased dramatically the scope of political activity in New Spain. The new charter established representative government at three levels: the municipality, the province, and the empire. Although the cortes that drafted the constitution included Americans as well as Europeans, the majority of deputies were Spaniards who, because they were principally concerned with the needs of the Peninsula, failed to understand the impact that the political changes would have on the New World. The constitution allowed cities and towns with a population of one thousand or more to form ayuntamientos.[7] The provision radically expanded the number of urban centers in New Spain that could establish municipalities. In ways we have yet to understand, political power was transferred from the center to the localities as large numbers of people were incorporated into the political process.

A new institution, the provincial deputation, which combined members elected locally with officials representing the imperial regime in Spain, governed the provinces. The new structure allowed Spanish provinces, already ruled by regional juntas, and rebellious American provinces to retain local administration while maintaining strong ties with the central government. With the creation of the provincial deputations, the cortes abolished the viceroyalty, transformed the audiencia from a quasi-administrative body into a high court, and divided the empire into provinces that dealt directly with the imperial government in Spain.[8] The once powerful office of viceroy was reduced to captain general of the Kingdom of New Spain and political chief of the Province of Mexico. In addition, New

---

1991): 2–3. See also idem, *En busca de un gobierno alterno: Los Guadalupes de México* (Mexico: Universidad Nacional Autónoma de México, 1992), 127–148.

[6]The best study of Mexican participation in the cortes is Nettie Lee Benson, ed., *Mexico and the Spanish Cortes, 1810–1822* (Austin: University of Texas Press, 1966). See, especially, Charles R. Berry, "The Election of Mexican Deputies to the Spanish Cortes, 1810–1822," in Benson, *Mexico and the Spanish Cortes*, 12–13.

[7]Guedea, *En busca de un gobierno alterno*, 180–186. On the constitutional ayuntamientos see Roger L. Cunniff, "Mexican Municipal Reform, 1810–1822," in Benson, *Mexico and the Spanish Cortes*, 59–86.

[8]On the provincial deputation see Nettie Lee Benson, *La Diputación Provincial y el federalismo mexicano* (Mexico: El Colegio de México, 1955).

Spaniards were allotted more than sixty seats in the cortes, giving them not only an important voice in empire-wide affairs but also another mechanism for restricting central authority and insisting upon home rule.

New Spaniards actively participated in the elections of 1812 and 1813. Because the elections were indirect, they involved large numbers of people at the parish, *partido*, and provincial level. Although the authorities in Mexico City, concerned because only Americans won, temporarily suspended the electoral process in 1812 on the grounds of irregularities, elections in other areas appear to have been carried out with little difficulty. Subsequently, in 1813, elections were renewed in the capital. In those years New Spaniards selected representatives to countless ayuntamientos, to six provincial deputations, and to the cortes in Spain.[9] The overwhelming majority of those elected were Americans who favored home rule. By 1814, when the king abolished the cortes and the constitution, colonial Mexicans had participated in several elections and many had served in constitutional ayuntamientos, in provincial deputations, and in the cortes in Spain. Their political experience would have profound and lasting effects in the country.

In their quest for home rule New Spaniards did not limit themselves to participation in the "legal" political process. After the Europeans seized control of the government of New Spain in 1808, the Americans began secretly organizing themselves. They formed clandestine groups that sought to wrest power from the *gachupines*. Although the authorities managed to uncover several conspiracies and maintained rigid control over the cities and towns of the viceroyalty,[10] Father Miguel Hidalgo and a group of conspirators unleashed a massive rural revolt on September 16, 1810. Because Hidalgo had inadvertently precipitated a class and race conflict, he found little support among New Spaniards.[11] His successors, Ignacio López

[9]Guedea, "La primeras elecciones populares en la ciudad de México," 1–28. See also idem, "El pueblo de México y las elecciones de 1812," in *La ciudad de México en la primera mitad del siglo XIX*, 2 vols., ed. Regina Hernández Franyuti (Mexico: Instituto de Investigaciones Dr. José María Luis Mora, 1994), 2:125–165; Guedea, *En busca de un gobierno alterno*, 127–231; Nettie Lee Benson, "The Contested Mexican Election of 1812," *Hispanic American Historical Review* 26 (August 1946): 336–350; and Rafael Alba, ed., *La Constitución de 1812 en la Nueva España*, 2 vols. (Mexico: Secretaría de Relaciones Exteriores, Imprenta Guerrero Hnos., 1912–1913).

[10]José Mariano Michelena, "Verdadero origen de la revolución de 1809 en el Departamento de Michoacán," in *Documentos históricos mexicanos*, 7 vols., 2d ed., ed. Genaro García (Mexico: Secretaría de Educación Pública, 1985), 1:467–471; Virginia Guedea, "Secret Societies during New Spain's Independence Movement" (Paper presented at the symposium New Interpretations of Mexican Independence, University of California, Berkeley, April 24, 1989).

[11]Hugh M. Hamill, Jr., *The Hidalgo Revolt: Prelude to Mexican Independence* (Gainesville: University of Florida Press, 1960); Virginia Guedea,

Rayón and Father José María Morelos, obtained greater backing by controlling their followers and by establishing a Junta Suprema Americana as the first step to forming a national government. Later they convened a congress to draft a Mexican constitution. The establishment of the junta, the convening of a congress, and the elections to that parliament were modeled on the institutions and practices of Spain. The insurgent leaders were responding to the new political reality occasioned by the Spanish constitutional system. Their actions appealed to the urban elites; many offered support, and a few openly joined the insurgent cause.[12]

The upheavals of the Independence period did not constitute a single movement. Instead, various groups and regions pursued their different interests. The conspiracies and political maneuverings of the urban elites differed widely from the aspirations of the rural masses. The emphasis placed by many historians on the insurgents and on agrarian issues has obscured the nature of the process of Independence. By focusing on rural conflict, they have overlooked the importance of the relationship between city and countryside in New Spain. Although for the most part an agrarian society, colonial Mexico was a region dominated by cities and towns. Landowners, large and small, lived in urban areas, not on their estates. Similarly, Indians congregated in corporate villages. Political power at all levels, therefore, resided in urban centers. The Constitution of 1812 not only reaffirmed the political role of the ayuntamientos but also expanded them to include towns that had not previously possessed municipal governments.[13] While the insurgents dominated much of the countryside, they could not hope to win unless they obtained support in the cities.

The abolition of the cortes and the constitution in 1814 was followed by the defeat of Morelos in 1815. Thereafter, the rebellion fragmented into a series of regional insurgencies.[14] Thus, no "national" movement existed that could attract the urban elites. Despite these reversals, New Spain's urban

---

José María Morelos y Pavón: Cronología (Mexico: Universidad Nacional Autónoma de México, 1981).

[12]Guedea, *En busca de un gobierno alterno*, 43–65, 67–125, 233–246. See also idem, "Los procesos electorales insurgentes," *Estudios de historia novohispana* 11 (1991): 201–249.

[13]"Lista de los Ayuntamientos Constitucionales establecidos en este Reyno . . . ," Archivo General de la Nación (hereafter cited as AGN), Ayuntamientos, vol. 120.

[14]Christon I. Archer has written extensively about the "fragmented insurgency"; see, among his essays, "Where Did All the Royalists Go? New Light on the Military Collapse of New Spain, 1810–1822," in *The Mexican and the Mexican-American Experience in the 19th Century*, ed. Jaime E. Rodríguez O. (Tempe, AZ: Bilingual Press, 1989), 24–43; and his " 'La Causa Buena': The Counterinsurgency Army of New Spain and the Ten Years' War," in Rodríguez, *The Independence of Mexico*, 85–108. See also Guedea, *En busca de un gobierno alterno*, 279–286.

elites continued to seek ways of gaining autonomy. The political ferment initiated by the constitutional system could not be easily contained. Secret groups, conspiracies, and clandestine political activities favoring home rule concerned the authorities of the viceroyalty.[15]

Once again, events in Spain transformed the situation in the colony. Early in 1820 liberals in the Peninsula rebelled against absolutism and restored the Constitution of 1812. When the news arrived in the viceroyalty in April, New Spaniards enthusiastically set about restoring the constitutional system. In the months that followed, ayuntamientos, from the Central American provinces in the south to Texas in the north, reported that in formal ceremonies they had sworn allegiance to the constitution and that they had restored or established constitutional ayuntamientos. Elections were held for constitutional ayuntamientos, provincial deputations, and the cortes.[16] Although they actively participated in the elections, New Spain's urban elites no longer believed that the cortes would accommodate their desire for home rule. Therefore, politically active New Spaniards engaged in intense debate about the future of their country in clandestine meetings, in secret organizations, and in *tertulias*.[17] Lucas Alamán and Manuel Gómez Pedraza, for example, have left us accounts of their participation in secret discussions in Puebla, Jalapa, and Veracruz before leaving for the cortes in Spain.[18]

As later events were to demonstrate, New Spaniards generally agreed on the need to establish an autonomous commonwealth within the Spanish empire. It was not an accident that plans for home rule, subsequently proposed in Madrid and in the viceroyalty, were similar. New Spain's deputies to the cortes presented a project for autonomy that took Canada as its model. The Spanish majority, however, rejected the proposal, which would have granted colonial Mexicans the home rule that they had been seeking since 1808. In New Spain, Colonel Agustín de Iturbide proclaimed the Plan of Iguala, which resembled the proposal rejected by the cortes in

---

[15]Guedea, *En busca de un gobierno alterno*, 287–358; Lucas Alamán, *Historia de México desde los primeros movimientos que prepararon su independencia en el año de 1808 hasta la época presente*, 5 vols. (Mexico: Fondo de Cultura Económica, 1985), 5:1–31.

[16]Berry, "Election of Mexican Deputies," 29–42; "Instrucciones para las elecciones a Cortes, 1820–1821," and "Elecciones de diputados, 1820," AGN, Ayuntamientos, vol. 168. Elections were held throughout New Spain, including many towns not listed as having the right to a constitutional ayuntamiento. See the reports in AGN, Ayuntamientos, vol. 120. Other reports on elections for 1820–1821 are located in AGN, Gobernación, Sin Sección, Caja 8.

[17]Alamán, *Historia de México*, 5:1–31.

[18]Ibid., 5:87–88; Manuel Gómez Pedraza, *Manifiesto que . . . ciudadano de la República de Méjico dedica a sus compatriotas, o sea una reseña de su vida pública*, 2d ed. (Guadalajara: Oficina de Brambillas, 1831).

Spain. The plan called for the establishment of a constitutional monarchy; it invited Fernando VII or, if he did not accept, a Spanish prince to head the government; it acknowledged the Constitution of 1812 and the statutes passed by the cortes as the laws of the land; it recognized the Catholic faith as the sole religion of the country; and it removed ethnic distinctions, declaring all New Spaniards, regardless of their place of birth, equal.[19]

When Spain refused to consider the proposals for autonomy, the leaders of New Spain declared independence and created the Mexican empire.[20] The newly emancipated Mexicans carefully followed Spanish precedents. They formed a Regency to serve as the executive and a Soberana Junta Provisional Gubernativa (Sovereign Provisional Governing Junta) to act as a legislative body until a cortes was convened. In addition, the provincial deputations and the constitutional ayuntamientos continued to govern their areas. Conflict quickly erupted between the executive and legislative branches of the new government. The Soberana Junta, like the First Constituent Congress which succeeded it, insisted on observing the procedures established by the Spanish Constitution of 1812, while Iturbide, first as president of the Regency and later as emperor, demanded substantial changes. The struggle centered on differing conceptions of sovereignty and national power. Following the precedent set by the Spanish cortes, Mexican legislators believed that the congress, as the representative of the nation, should be supreme. Iturbide, on the other hand, was convinced that he represented the national will because he had achieved independence. Like Fernando VII before him, Iturbide disbanded the congress in 1822, establishing a Junta Nacional Instituyente which he hoped would follow his dictates. The new political arrangement proved unworkable. As had occurred earlier in Spain, discontent led to rebellion in the provinces, ultimately forcing the emperor to abdicate in

[19]"Exposición presentada a las Cortes por los diputados de ultramar en la sesión de junio de 1821," in Alamán, *Historia de México*, 5, Apendice, 49–65; Agustín de Iturbide, "Plan de la Independencia de la América Septentrional," in *1810–1821: Documentos básicos para la independencia*, ed. Rene Cárdenas Barrios (Mexico: Ediciones del Sector Eléctrico, 1979), 274–286. Plans to establish autonomous monarchies within the Spanish empire had been circulating since the late eighteenth century. It is evident that, by 1821, New Spain's elites had reached a consensus on the question. Iturbide's merit is that he made the concept his own when he proclaimed the Plan of Iguala. On the question see, for example, Nettie Lee Benson, "Iturbide y los planes de independencia," *Historia Mexicana* 2, no. 3 (January–March 1953): 439–446.

[20]See the documents published by Carlos Herrejón Peredo, ed., *Actas de la Diputación Provincial de Nueva España, 1820–1821* (Mexico: Cámara de Diputados, 1985); and by Roberto Olagaray, ed., *Colección de Documentos Históricos Mexicanos*, 4 vols. (Mexico: Antigua Imprenta de Murgía, 1924), vol. 2.

March 1823.[21] By then the political situation in Mexico had changed so dramatically that the Mexico City-based elites could no longer control the nation.

The growth of political participation during the years 1820 to 1823 is astounding. The Galería de Gobernación in the Archivo General de la Nación (AGN) in Mexico City contains thousands of uncatalogued *legajos*, many of them dealing with this period. Countless letters, reports, requests, complaints, and other material record the intensity of political activity in the country.[22]

Information was disseminated nationwide with amazing rapidity. Hundreds of *legajos* in the Galería de Gobernación contain laws, decrees, circulars, and information sent throughout the land. Typical is an 1821 *legajo* with a circular informing officials and corporations that the Soberana Junta is to be addressed as "Su Magestad." The legajo contains the circular and hundreds of responses from throughout Mexico indicating that the information had been received and distributed. Some letters state that the official had received thirty, forty, sixty, or one hundred copies of the document. Others declare that additional copies had been printed for local distribution. By comparing the date of the circular with that of the most distant response, we can determine that information traveled to the furthermost point in the nation within one week.[23] To ensure rapid communications, the independent government issued a decree in 1822 dismissing any official who did not properly disseminate information within three days of its receipt.[24]

[21]See Jaime E. Rodríguez O., "The Struggle for Dominance: The Legislature versus the Executive in Early Mexico" (Paper presented at the conference The Mexican Wars of Independence, the Empire, and the Early Republic, University of Calgary, April 4–5, 1991). The initial conflict between Iturbide and the Soberana Junta is clearly reflected in the minutes of the junta. See *Diario de las sesiones de la Soberana Junta Provisional Gubernativa del Imperio Mexicano* (Mexico: Imprenta Imperial de Alejandro Valdés, 1821), 6–7, 17–19. The clashes with the First Constituent Congress are found in the *Actas del Congreso Constituyente Mexicano*, 3 vols. (Mexico: Imprenta de Alejandro Valdés, 1823). José Barragán y Barragán has written a sympathetic analysis of the activities of the various legislative bodies during the period from 1820 to 1824; see his *Introducción al federalismo* (Mexico: Universidad Nacional Autónoma de México, 1978). Timothy E. Anna presents the pro-Iturbide view in *The Mexican Empire of Iturbide* (Lincoln: University of Nebraska Press, 1990).

[22]The documents are found in two large sections of the Galería 5, Gobernación, at the AGN: Legajos and Sin Sección.

[23]See the expedientes in AGN, Gobernación, Legajo 26.

[24]Decree, April 26, 1822, AGN, Gobernación, Legajo 17, expediente 6. The expediente includes the immediate response from more than one hundred officials.

After 1820 the printing press became the indispensable instrument of Mexican politics. Important notices, decrees, laws, circulars, minutes of special meetings, reports of elections, statements from prominent politicians, and other matters of interest were printed almost immediately both in the capital and in the provinces. Politically active Mexicans learned of significant events within days of their occurrence; they possessed copies of important documents, and they made certain that they took advantage of their rights. The AGN is filled with requests from all parts of the country for clarification of articles x, y, and z of specific decrees and with inquiries as to their relationship to earlier laws. The provincials were particularly concerned about electoral procedures.[25] Indeed, the secretary of internal and external affairs received numerous reports about electoral disputes in provincial centers.[26]

The voluminous documentation indicates that the ayuntamientos had become the focus of Mexican political life. The major provincial cities, for example, took the lead in expanding the number of provincial deputations in the country. There had been six in 1814. When the constitution was restored in 1820, New Spaniards insisted on increasing the number. Provincial deputations grew to fifteen in 1820, eighteen in 1822, and twenty-three in 1823, when they began the process of converting themselves into states.[27]

The documents demonstrate a clear progression in the nature of the political discourse. The writings, even those from small Indian towns, are quite sophisticated. They demonstrate wide-ranging knowledge of events both in the Old World and the New, and familiarity with the political thought of the time. Many letters and reports are peppered with Latin expressions and citations from political theorists, particularly French authors. Before Independence, in 1820 and 1821, the localities extol the virtues of the constitutional system. They also insist on the importance of "la patria," "la nación," "nuestra tierra," "América," and "América Septentrional."[28] It is evident that they had developed a strong sense of nationality. After Independence, the documents glorify Iturbide as the liberator, but they also emphasize the significance of "el imperio

[25]See the queries in AGN, Gobernación, Sin Sección, Caja 12, expediente 7. All are dated 1821.

[26]See, for example, the disputes located in AGN, Gobernación, Legajo 1832 (1), expediente 1.

[27]On the activities of the ayuntamientos see, for example, AGN, Gobernación, Sin Sección, Caja 13, expediente 6, and Caja 9, expediente 10. On the activities of the provincial deputations see Benson, *La Diputación Provincial*, 66–198.

[28]See AGN, Gobernación, Sin Sección, Caja 9, Caja 12, and Caja 13; and AGN, Gobernación, Legajo 1578, expediente 1.

mexicano," "Anahuac," and "América."[29] In 1823, following Iturbide's abdication, the documents exalt the Plan of Casa Mata, which led to the emperor's fall, as well as the glories of liberty.[30] Late in 1822, but especially in 1823, the writings discuss the importance of provincial government. From Chiapas in the south to Texas in the north, the ayuntamientos insist on the absolute necessity of local government. Many lengthy reports argue that only at the provincial level could Mexicans obtain the kind of responsive government they required. The Ayuntamiento of Mérida, for example, indicated that in so vast a country, with different climates and different conditions, it was impossible to meet provincial needs with uniform laws.[31] The Ayuntamiento of Béjar maintained that only local officials could understand regional requirements. And Mérida added that the provinces had to control their representatives because a deputy who resided in Mexico City too long would become a *capitalino* and forget his region.

Provincial Mexicans were convinced by 1823 that only federalism could keep the nation united. They insisted on the sovereignty of the provinces, but they also agreed that the nation must not fragment. Every ayuntamiento affirmed that provincial sovereignty did not conflict with national unity. They asserted that the country required a "centro de unión."[32] Some listed in detail the division of power between the national government and the regions. Guadalajara, for example, declared that the nation only had the right to appoint general officers, while the provinces should name those with the rank of colonel and below. Similarly, Mérida insisted that the national government could only propose bishops; all other clerical appointments were reserved for the states.[33]

In those circumstances, a federalist system was the only form of government acceptable to most Mexicans. During February and March 1823, when they had opposed Iturbide, the provincial deputations informed each other of their actions and began to discuss the manner in which they should create a national government. On March 10, Puebla invited each province to send two delegates to a convention to form a provisional

---

[29]See, for example, AGN, Gobernación, Sin Sección, Caja 16 and Caja 23; and AGN, Historia, vol 429. Javier Ocampo's otherwise excellent work, *Las ideas de un día: El pueblo mexicano ante la consumación de su Independencia* (Mexico: El Colegio de México, 1969), has created the false impression that national enthusiasm focused solely on Iturbide because the author limited himself to an analysis of that episode.

[30]See AGN, Gobernación, Sin Sección, Caja 43, expediente 9; also Caja 44, expediente 7; and Caja 48, expediente 30.

[31]Junta Gubernativa de Mérida to Secretary of Relations, July 12, 1823, AGN, Gobernación, Sin Sección, Caja 43, expediente 54.

[32]See, for example, the reports in AGN, Gobernación, Sin Sección, Caja 43, expediente 53.

[33]AGN, Gobernación, Sin Sección, Caja 43, expediente 1 and expediente 5.

government. Three days later Michoacán proposed that representatives from Michoacán, Querétaro, San Luis Potosí, and the Eastern Interior Provinces meet in Querétaro to establish a national government, a suggestion it abandoned when it learned of Puebla's invitation. The majority of provinces sent representatives to Puebla, but before most arrived, Iturbide reconvened the First Constituent Congress and then abdicated. A rump session, calling itself the Junta of Puebla, recognized the reconvened congress but only for the purpose of convoking a new constituent congress. The other provinces agreed.[34]

The provinces of Mexico insisted on electing a new constituent congress in order to ensure their own autonomy. They rejected the First Constituent Congress's claim, based on the actions of the Spanish cortes, that it was the repository of national sovereignty. Instead, the provinces held that they themselves possessed sovereignty and that they were relinquishing a portion of that sovereignty to create a national government. In addition, they insisted on limiting the power of their representatives. As Zacatecas declared: "The deputies to the future congress cannot constitute the nation as they deem convenient; but [only] under a system of a federal republic."[35] Yucatán was even more explicit when it decreed that "the elected deputies are granted only the power . . . to constitute the nation in a government that is republican, representative, and federal."[36] The provinces of Guadalajara and Guanajuato joined Zacatecas and Yucatán in placing restrictions upon their representatives to the new constituent congress.

The provinces considered themselves the arbiters of the nation in mid-1823. Oaxaca, Yucatán, Jalisco, and Zacatecas installed constituent legislatures while others, declaring themselves sovereign and independent states, created provincial governments. Most sent commissioners to Mexico City to ensure that the First Constituent Congress obeyed their wishes. That body, however, refused to acknowledge provincial authority. Instead, it attempted to impose its will upon the country by force.[37] Rather than capitulating, the provinces raised militias to defend their territories, joining forces to oppose the national army. The urban elites, who dominated the congress, ultimately capitulated, declaring support for the federal system and issuing instructions for convening a new constituent congress. Nevertheless, the outgoing congress insisted that the new one would retain supreme

[34]Benson, *La Diputación Provincial*, 85 and passim; Puebla, *Acta de la Junta de Puebla sobre la reinstalación del congreso mexicano* (Puebla: Oficina de D. Pedro de la Rosa, 1823). See also Efraín Castro Morales, *El federalismo en Puebla* (Puebla: Gobierno del Estado de Puebla, 1987), 71–102.

[35]*Aguila Mexicana*, August 22, 1823.

[36]Ibid., August 17, 1823.

[37]Jaime E. Rodríguez O., "The Struggle for the Nation: The First Centralist-Federalist Conflict in Mexico," *The Americas* 49, no. 1 (July 1992): 1–22.

authority; it declared in its *convocatoria* that "each and every [deputy] shall possess very ample powers to constitute the Mexican Nation in the manner he considers best for its general well-being, maintaining inalterable the foundations of religion, independence, and union."[38]

The Second Constituent Congress, which met on November 7, 1823, faced very different circumstances than its predecessor. Local interests, both at the ayuntamiento and at the provincial levels, insisted on determining the form of government that the nation should possess. Although most favored federalism, a few still hoped that a centralist system might be established.[39] But even federalists were divided; some preferred a strong federation while others favored a weak confederation. Most important, the level of public interest and expectation was quite high. After several years of intense political participation, Mexicans insisted upon a voice in the formation of their government. Indeed, many appeared ready to use force, if necessary, to obtain their goals.

From its inception, the Second Constituent Congress faced the thorny question of the limitations placed on the delegates by the provinces of Jalisco, Zacatecas, Guanajuato, and Yucatán. The committee to verify the credentials of the deputies had addressed the issue on November 4. Some members argued that the provinces could not restrict the authority of their delegates and, therefore, they questioned the credentials of the deputies with limited powers. The majority, however, maintained that those deputies should be seated because they represented four million inhabitants, the majority of the nation's population, and because they believed that the restrictions on their authority would not limit the congress's deliberations. José Miguel Ramos Arizpe of Coahuila carried the day when he convinced the delegates that their priority should be to constitute the nation.[40]

Since the provinces, most of which now called themselves states, had determined that Mexico must have a federal republic, debate in the congress focused on the critical issue of who was sovereign: the nation or the states. On this question the delegates were divided into four factions. Extreme defenders of states' rights, such as Juan de Dios Cañedo of Jalisco, argued that only the states possessed sovereignty, a portion of which they collectively ceded to the union in order to form a national government. This interpretation meant that the states could subsequently reclaim what they had relinquished. Their opponents, men such as Servando Teresa de Mier of

---

[38]Article 73, "Decreto de 17 de junio de 1823—Bases para las elecciones del nuevo congreso," Manuel Dublán and José María Lozano, *Legislación mexicana*, 34 vols. (Mexico: Dublán y Lozano Hijos, 1876–1904), 1:651–659.

[39]Carlos María de Bustamante, *Diario histórico de México*, 3 vols. (Mexico: Instituto Nacional de Antropología, 1980–1984), 1:pt. 2:103–119.

[40]Mexico, Cámara de Diputados, *Crónicas del Acta Constitutiva* (Mexico: Cámara de Diputados, 1974), 45–47.

Nuevo León, believed that only the nation was sovereign. Although the country was organized into provinces (or states) for political purposes, the people, and not the states, possessed sovereignty. The deputies, therefore, did not represent the states but rather the people who constituted the nation. This argument signified that the congress, as the representative of the Mexican people, possessed greater power and authority than the state legislatures. The claim reasserted the view that had prevailed in Cádiz in 1812. Midway between these extremes stood those who, like Ramos Arizpe, believed that the national government and the states must share sovereignty. Although these moderates favored states' rights, they nevertheless thought that the national government had to command sufficient power to function effectively. Finally, a tiny minority of centralists, such as Carlos María de Bustamante, representing the state of Mexico, opposed federalism, arguing that the country needed a strong national government if it were to prosper.

As one of its first acts, the Second Constituent Congress appointed a committee to prepare a draft of a constitution, or an *acta constitutiva*. The committee, composed of Ramos Arizpe, Cañedo, Miguel Argüelles of Veracruz, Rafael Mangino of Puebla, Tomás Vargas of San Luis Potosí, José de Jesús Huerta of Jalisco, and Manuel Crescencio Rejón of Yucatán, agreed to submit the draft within a few days. It was possible to complete the draft of the charter rapidly because proposals for a constitution had been widely debated throughout the country. In addition, the deputies were highly educated men, some of whom had participated in elected government at various levels, and a few, like Ramos Arizpe, had served in the cortes in Spain and had even helped draft the Constitution of 1812. Indeed, Ramos Arizpe had been working on a federal constitution for some time.[41]

The committee submitted the proposed *acta* on November 20. Because it was modeled on the Constitution of 1812, most of its articles were based on the Spanish document and a few were copied verbatim from that charter. The proposed *acta* consisted of forty articles. Article 5 established a federal republic, while Article 9 stated: "The supreme power of the Mexican Federation is divided . . . [among] legislative, executive, and judicial [branches]." The legislature consisted of two houses, a chamber of deputies and a senate. Executive authority was vested in a president, who was assisted by a vice president, and judicial power was granted to an independent judiciary consisting of "a supreme court of justice, and the tribunals and *juzgados* which each state establishes." Article 3 declared: "The religion of the Mexican Nation is and shall be perpetually the Roman, Catholic, and Apostolic [Church]. The Nation will protect [the Church] with wise and just laws and prohibits the exercise of any other [religion]." The *acta*, unlike the Spanish document, did not grant exclusive sovereignty to the nation because

[41]Benson, *La Diputación Provincial*, 192–201.

the states also claimed sovereignty. Accordingly, Article 6 stated: "Its integral parts are independent, free, and sovereign states, regarding their internal administration and government exclusively."[42]

While relying on the Spanish experience, the congressmen adapted it to reflect Mexican reality. José Miguel Guridi y Alcocer of Tlaxcala, for example, explained that ever since he had served on the constitutional commission in the Spanish cortes he had insisted on maintaining that sovereignty resided *radically* in the nation, by which he meant the nation could not lose its sovereignty.[43] Although some deputies questioned Guridi y Alcocer's wording, the majority approved his proposal. Cañedo, however, challenged the need for an article declaring national sovereignty. He recommended "that the article be deleted, because if a republican, federal government is adopted, and each state is sovereign, as a later article [Article 6] asserts, it is impossible to conceive how sovereignty, which is the origin and source of authority and power and, therefore, is one, can be divided among the many states. That is why the first constitution of the United States [the Articles of Confederation] . . . does not mention national sovereignty. And, therefore, . . . Article 1 which discusses the nation should not be approved because it is not appropriate in the system which we now have."[44] Thus, the issue of sovereignty remained at heart a question of the division of power between the national and the state governments. Representatives such as Cañedo rejected the notion of national sovereignty, preferring instead the creation of sovereign states. In their discussions, the members of the congress who favored a loose confederation invoked as examples not only the Articles of Confederation of the United States but also the traditional Habsburg notion of independent kingdoms federated under the authority of the monarch.

Other delegates, who argued that only the nation could be sovereign, challenged the proponents of state sovereignty. Because these men stressed the need to endow the national government with sufficient power to sustain national interests, they have often been confused with centralists.[45] Although a tiny minority advocated centralism, most favored a strong federal system. Mier, the group's outstanding spokesman, argued that people wrongly considered him a centralist, an error that arose from an unnecessarily restrictive definition of federalism. He indicated that federalism

---

[42]"Acta Constitutiva de la Nación Mexicana," in *Crónicas del Acta Constitutiva*, 101–108.

[43]*Crónicas del Acta Constitutiva*, 269.

[44]Ibid., 270.

[45]Barragán y Barragán, *Introducción al federalismo*, 197–198.

existed in many forms: Germany, Switzerland, Holland, and the United States were federations, yet each was different.[46]

Father Mier advocated the formation of a federalist system suited to Mexico. He believed that local realities precluded the adoption of the extreme form of federation championed by states' righters. He declared: "I have always been in favor of a federation, but a reasonable and moderate federation. . . . I have always believed in a medium between the lax federation of the United States, whose defects many writers have pointed out, . . . and the dangerous concentration [of power] in Colombia and Peru."[47] In Mier's view, Mexico needed a strong federal system because a state of war with Spain still existed, because the Holy Alliance threatened to intervene, and because Mexico required an energetic national government to lead it during the critical early years of nationhood. For these reasons, he subsequently voted in favor of Article 5, which established a federal republic, while opposing Article 6, which granted sovereignty to the states.[48]

Neither the advocates of states' rights, like Cañedo, nor the proponents of national sovereignty, like Mier, triumphed. Instead, a compromise emerged: shared sovereignty, as advocated by moderates such as Ramos Arizpe. Throughout the debates, the moderates argued that although the nation was sovereign, the states should control their internal affairs. The group saw no conflict between Article 3, which declared that sovereignty resided in the nation, and Article 6, which granted sovereignty to the states on internal matters. They successfully maneuvered to pass both articles. A coalition of the proponents of national sovereignty, the advocates of shared sovereignty, and a few centralists obtained a large majority vote for Article 3. To secure passage of Article 6, those favoring compromise succeeded in having the question brought to the floor in two parts. The first vote on the section of Article 6 that stated that the states were *free and independent* to manage their own affairs passed by a wide margin, since the wording pleased all federalist groups. Only seven centralist deputies opposed the measure. The congress then entertained the section of Article 6 that declared that the states were *sovereign*. The coalition divided on this issue: Father Mier and his supporters joined the centralists in voting against it. Nevertheless, the proponents of states' rights and those who believed in shared sovereignty possessed enough strength to pass the measure by forty-one to twenty-eight votes.[49]

[46]Nettie Lee Benson, "Servando Teresa de Mier, Federalist," *Hispanic American Historical Review* 28, no. 4 (November 1948): 514–525.

[47]Consult Mier's speech in *Crónicas del Acta Constitutiva*, 280–294.

[48]Ibid., 338, 367.

[49]Ibid., 272, 338, 367.

The compromise to share sovereignty did not settle the question of the division of powers within the national government. Although all agreed on the traditional concept of separation of powers among the legislative, executive, and judicial branches, most congressmen believed that the legislature should be dominant. Recent Spanish and Mexican experience fostered a distrust of executive power. The Constitution of 1812 granted the cortes dominance while restricting the Crown. Similarly, the Constitution of Apatzingán severely limited Morelos's pretensions to supreme power. Although that insurgent leader never had the opportunity to contend with the rebel congress, Fernando VII abolished the cortes and the constitution in 1814. Later, the Soberana Junta and the First Constituent Congress clashed with Iturbide, first as president of the Regency and subsequently as emperor. As a result, Mexicans harbored deep suspicions of, and a strong hostility toward, the tendency of leaders to seek unbridled power.

After Iturbide abdicated in March 1823, the restored First Constituent Congress grappled with the problem of executive power. Well aware of the "tyrannies" of Fernando VII of Spain and Agustín I of Mexico, legislators were reluctant to grant power to the executive branch. Some searched for a term which, while recognizing the functions, would not include the word "executive" in the title. In the end the congress compromised by creating a triumvirate called the Supreme Executive Power, who would alternate the presidency among them on a monthly basis.[50] On March 31 the congress elected Generals Nicolás Bravo, Guadalupe Victoria, and Pedro Celestino Negrete to serve as the the Supreme Executive Power. Later, it selected José Mariano Michelena, José Miguel Domínguez, and Vicente Guerrero as substitutes for Bravo, Victoria, and Negrete, who were in the field with their troops. Like the Spanish cortes, the Mexican congress believed that the executive branch existed solely for the purpose of carrying out the wishes of the legislature.

The draft of the *acta constitutiva*, however, proposed that executive power be granted "to an individual with the name of President of the Mexican Federation, who must be a citizen by birth, and 35 years of age." The proposal led to a heated debate that transcended the former divisions between states' righters and strong nationalists. While Cañedo supported Ramos Arizpe in favoring a single executive, others, including Rejón and Guridi y Alcocer, insisted on the need to weaken executive power by establishing a plural executive. In an attempt to mollify the opposition, Ramos Arizpe proposed that the president govern with the advice of a council of government. But that was not sufficient to pacify the opposition, which consisted of the majority of the congress.

---

[50]*Diario de las sesiones del Congreso constituyente*, 4 vols. (Mexico: Oficina de Valdés, 1823), 4:48 (*sic*, in error for 84)–122; Alamán, *Historia de México*, 5:759–760.

The opponents of a single executive presented several proposals. Demetrio Castillo of Oaxaca suggested that a president, a vice president, and an alternate, or *designado*, govern. Each would have a vote, but the president "would decide." Rejón, instead, recommended that three individuals form the Supreme Executive Power; one would be replaced every year so that a member would always possess seniority, but no one would serve for more than three years. Guridi y Alcocer proposed that executive power be conferred on two persons. He argued that the best solution was to merge the experiences of the United States, Spain, and ancient Rome. Therefore, he urged that the two members of the executive power be backed by two alternates who might resolve any difference that arose between the two members of the executive.[51]

Although the congress repeatedly rejected the suggestion that executive power be vested in one person, the commission continued to insist on a single executive. The core of the argument in favor was that only an individual could provide the unity of purpose and the speed necessary to carry out the functions of the executive branch. In short, the argument was one of efficiency, while the opponents expressed the fear, based on recent history, that a single executive could become a despot.

The revolt of General José María Lobato on January 20, 1824, however, changed the nature of the debate on the executive branch. The rebels demanded the dismissal of Spaniards from government jobs and their expulsion from the country. They also insisted that two of the three triumvirs, Michelena and Domínguez, resign. The reason for this demand remains unclear. Both men were heroes of the early Independence movement. Michelena had also fought in the Peninsula against the French and represented New Spain in the cortes. Although he had once favored a constitutional monarchy, Michelena was known to have been an implacable enemy of Fernando VII and Agustín I. Since he was acting president of the Supreme Executive Power when the rebellion began, it is possible that the uprising was directed in part against the attempt to create a single executive which Michelena, as a close ally of Ramos Arizpe, favored.

The plural executive, and the division of power within the government, hampered action against the rebels. Lobato managed to win the support of the garrisons in the capital, and the government seemed on the verge of capitulation when the Supreme Executive Power convinced the congress to declare Lobato an outlaw and to grant the executive branch sufficient power to quell the rebellion.[52] The Lobato revolt persuaded many

---

[51]*Crónicas del Acta Constitutiva*, 447–450.

[52]Documents on the Lobato revolt are published in José María Bocanegra, *Memorias para la historia de México independiente, 1822–1846*, 3 vols. (Mexico: Fondo de Cultura Económica, 1987), 1:339–343, 338–339. Other documents concerning the revolt appear in *El Iris de Jalisco*, February 2, 9, 11,

congressmen that they should not so weaken the executive that it could not act decisively in time of danger. The incident also convinced the congress of the unwieldiness of the plural executive, and members compromised to complete the *acta constitutiva*. The article on the executive stated that "supreme executive power would be vested by the constitution in an individual or individuals which that [charter] would name." Eventually, the congress opted for a president and vice president.

The creation of a single executive, however, did not mean that the congress had accepted a strong presidency. Most Mexicans continued to favor congressional superiority. The Constitution of 1824 created a quasi-parliamentary system, making the secretaries of state responsible to the congress. The Mexican charter, like the Spanish constitution, severely restricted the power of the chief executive. Consequently, the secretary of internal and external affairs tended to act as a quasi-prime minister. The presidency remained weak until the latter nineteenth century, when first Benito Juárez and then Porfirio Díaz strengthened that office.

After months of debate, the congress ratified the constitution on October 4, 1824. The Constitution of 1824, like the *acta constitutiva*, was not only modeled on the Spanish Constitution of 1812 but also often repeated sections verbatim.[53] This imitation was only natural since New Spaniards had served in the cortes and had helped draft the Spanish charter. Indeed, many Mexicans considered the Cádiz constitution *their* first charter. But it would be an error to consider the Constitution of 1824 a carbon copy of the 1812 document. Events in Mexico, particularly the assertion of states' rights by the former provinces, forced the congress to frame a constitution to meet the unique circumstances of the nation. The principal innovations—republicanism, federalism, and a presidency—were adopted to address Mexico's new reality. Far from being unrealistic and utopian, as is sometimes alleged, the 1824 charter sought to resolve the critical issues affecting the nation.

The framers of the constitution carefully considered the needs of their country. They granted the states the important role demanded by the regions, and that accommodation contributed significantly to maintaining national unity. As Nettie Lee Benson has indicated, it is no accident that despite numerous centrifugal forces, Mexico remained united while Central and

---

1824; Bustamante, *Diario histórico de México*, 2: (January 23, 1824), 17; (January 24, 1824), 17–18. See also the discussion in Mexico, Cámara de Diputados, *Historia parlamentaria: Sesiones secretas*, 2 vols. (Mexico: Instituto de Investigaciones Legislativas, Cámara de Diputados, 1982), 1:172–179, as well as the comments of Miguel Beruete, "Diario de México" (January 25, 26, 27, 28, 29, 30, and February 1, 2, 1824), Tulane University Library.

[53]Mexico, Cámara de Diputados, *Crónicas de la Constitución Federal de 1824*, 2 vols. (Mexico: Cámara de Diputados, 1974), 1:81–109.

South America fragmented into many smaller nations. Unfortunately, the Mexican statesmen could not contain the tremendous forces unleashed by over a decade of political change. The First Federal Republic endured mass demonstrations, riots, and political violence at a time when representative institutions were in their infancy. Given the rise of localism and the intense political participation throughout the country, it is doubtful that any other form of government would have better suited the needs of the nation. Indeed, it seems evident that none other was possible.

The Making of a Fait Accompli: Mexico and the Provincias Internas, 1776–1846

Barbara A. Tenenbaum

WHEN THE VICEROYALTY OF NEW SPAIN became independent in 1821, its territory ranged from the northernmost outposts of the Spanish empire in North America to the limits of Central America down to present-day Panama. Until 1823 all of that territory remained part of the new Mexican nation. With the fall of Emperor Agustín I, however, Central America, with the significant exception of Chiapas and Soconusco, broke with Mexico to form its own national entities while the far north continued as part of the Mexican republic. This essay challenges historians to reexamine the nature of that union by exploring the financial relationships between the northern region and Mexico City from 1776 until 1846.

Almost from the very beginning of their colonization of New Spain, Spanish officials, like the Aztecs who had preceded them, recognized that the farther the Crown traveled from Mexico City, the more difficulties it would encounter in governing that territory. The reasons are obvious. Lacking the modern enhancements to state building such as railroads and the telegraph, communications and transportation from remote areas in the north to the center would be extremely difficult. In addition, those areas were substantially underpopulated due to frequent attacks by marauding Indians.

Although some of the territory yielded rich mineral resources, in the main the Spanish Crown colonized the far north in order to provide a line of defense against English, French, or Russian efforts in the region. From the

AUTHOR'S NOTE: The writer gratefully acknowledges the invaluable assistance of Professor John Jay TePaske, Duke University, in reformulating this essay and in particular his personal communication, June 9, 1991. She wishes to thank the editor of this volume for his helpful comments and also Lic. Carlos Rodríguez for his research in the Archivo General de la Nación, Mexico City, on her behalf.

very beginning of Spanish settlement in New Spain, conquistadores acting independently with bands of Hispanicized Indians and mestizos and, more frequently as time passed, priests accompanied by Crown officials were sent to explore (some might say colonize) ever farther northward in search of souls, riches, and new locations for fortresses. For example, Spain in 1565 founded the first European city in the present-day United States, San Agustín, and constructed forts as far north as South Carolina when it sent Pedro Menéndez de Avilés, the captain of the Indies Fleet, on a mission to eliminate the French settlement at Fort Caroline in present-day Florida.

By the eighteenth century, however, the situation in the area known as América Septentrional (North America) had become increasingly precarious. First, few Spaniards and Mexicans, including Hispanicized Indians, had chosen to colonize so far away. Second, Spanish sovereignty over the area was extremely difficult and costly to maintain. And third, the viceroy in Mexico City was simply too far removed to handle regional areas reasonably and with dispatch. Two almost concurrent events conspired to complicate matters even further. In 1767 the Crown, following closely on the heels of its Portuguese neighbor, expelled the Jesuit order from all its dominions. That forced the Dominican order to take over the Jesuit missions in Arizona and Baja California so that the Franciscans, under the leadership of Fray Junípero Serra, could continue founding missions up the coast of California all the way north to San Francisco (1776).

In 1776 colonial North America began a series of massive territorial readjustments. Thirteen of the British colonies declared themselves in revolt while Spain moved to strengthen its hold over its empire. In addition to creating a fourth viceroyalty in La Plata, Secretarío de Estado del Despacho Universal de Indias José de Gálvez formed a new administrative unit, the Provincias Internas (Interior Provinces), to fortify royal control over América Septentrional. The new *comandante general* of the region, headquartered in Arizpe in present-day Sonora, was to administer an area that then included the *gobiernos* of Sinaloa and Sonora, Alta and Baja California, Nuevo México, Nueva Vizcaya (present-day Chihuahua and Durango), Coahuila, and Texas, a territory slightly larger than the rest of the viceroyalty. According to Gálvez's instructions, the new area was to be under the jurisdiction of Teodoro de Croix, separate and apart from the control of Viceroy Antonio María de Bucareli, much to the latter's disgust.

The Crown would change its mind four separate times before the War for Independence in New Spain itself halted the process. In 1786, Spanish authorities enlarged the Provincias Internas by adding Nuevo León and Nuevo Santander (present-day Tamaulipas) but put the entire unit back squarely under viceregal control. In effect, then, even though these two *gobiernos* were added, they were never administered like the original territory designated under the Provincias Internas. The new arrangement reasserted viceregal control over the entire territory now split into three parts with the *comandante general* of the Provincias Internas having authority only over Sonora and the Californias, while lesser officials were put in charge of the center (Nueva Vizcaya and Nuevo México) and of the east (Coahuila, Texas, Nuevo León, and Nuevo Santander). In the following year, 1787, the area was divided into Occidente and Oriente, both of which remained under viceregal control. On November 23, 1792, the Crown ordered that a *comandante general* would oversee a smaller Provincias Internas, now without Nuevo León and Nuevo Santander. The viceroy himself would control those two territories together with the Californias. Finally, Spanish officials reversed themselves one more time and divided the entire original area into Occidente and Oriente under the viceroy's command. That solution lasted from 1811 until Independence.[1]

The five different governing schemes put in place from 1776 to 1811 reflect much more than the respective power of viceroys and *comandantes generales*. They emphasize the basic difficulty in administering an area which, according to María del Carmen Velázquez, many Mexicans at that time considered a colony of central Mexico.[2] Indeed, in 1813 when the Congress of Chilpancingo discussed the territorial composition of the eventual independent nation of Mexico, its members did not include the "provinces" of Texas, Nuevo Santander, Nuevo México, and the Californias in their consensus concerning which territories would rightfully be included in the new state.[3] And no wonder. If Peter Gerhard's estimates are even a reflection of true population, then the Mexican residents in those areas—Texas, Nuevo Santander, Nuevo México, and the Californias—hardly amounted to 22.7 percent of the total residing in the Provincias Internas, to say nothing of the small percentage they represented of "Mexico" as a whole. When Nuevo Santander is omitted, then the other three territories did not contain even 10 percent of those living in the Provincias Internas itself.[4]

---

[1]In order to maintain consistency, this essay excludes the *gobiernos* of Nuevo Santander and Nuevo León from its discussion of the Provincias Internas since they were added after 1776 and did not remain part of the administrative unit for very long. Edmundo O'Gorman, *Historia de las divisiones territoriales de México* (Mexico: Editorial Porrúa, 1966), 15–19; Peter Gerhard, *The North Frontier of New Spain* (Princeton: Princeton University Press, 1982), introduction.

[2]María del Carmen Velázquez, *La frontera norte y la experiencia colonial* (Mexico: Secretaría de Relaciones Exteriores, Archivo Histórico Diplomático Mexicano 11, 1982), 7.

[3]O'Gorman, *Historia de las divisiones*, 32. It is, however, worth remembering that Texas was entitled to send a deputy to the cortes of 1812. See Nettie Lee Benson, "Texas's Failure to Send a Deputy to the Spanish Cortes, 1810–1812," *Southwestern Historical Quarterly* 64 (July 1960): 1–22.

[4]Gerhard, *The North Frontier*, 24.

Given the tiny number of people there, it should not be surprising that those gathered at Chilpancingo could so easily forget about territory so far to the north. After all, for central Mexico, none of those places had substantial mines such as those in Guanajuato or Zacatecas or any other resource that could be considered profitable; moreover, they required considerable financial help. But the dismissal of the north among those at that meeting perhaps had deeper roots. The common perception in central Mexico at the time, as Velázquez notes, was that the Provincias Internas as a whole, "lejos de reportarle beneficios económicos le eran gravosas" (far from providing any economic benefits, were a burden [on the national treasury]).[5]

However, reports from the *cajas reales* (royal treasuries) in the Provincias Internas do not confirm that assumption. The *real hacienda* of Mexico City only began to send money there in 1769. Up until that time the viceregal administration had founded only one branch of the royal treasury, Durango (1596), for the entire northern frontier. Since the other four *cajas* appeared much later—beginning with Los Alamos, Rosario, and Cosalá in 1770, followed by Arizpe in 1781, Chihuahua in 1785, and finally Saltillo in 1794—it is impossible to know how these areas were financed prior to the establishment of their own *cajas reales*. Yet the reports do reveal how the keepers of the central treasury in Mexico City understood the subsidies paid to the Provincias Internas. Instead of noting the origin of the funds with the rubric *remitido de la caja de México* or citing *otras cajas* as they did elsewhere, royal officials recorded the figures under the term *situados internos*. This term, so similar to *situados ultramarinos* or *situados cubanos*, reflects a comparable attitude toward those payments as if the northern territories were somewhat foreign and separate despite their contiguity.

The figures for the *situado* payments are quite suggestive. If those amounts are expressed as percentages of the total collections for any given year from 1769 to 1810, then we find that only from 1769 to 1774, in 1782, and in 1786 are the payments greater than the amounts collected in the area itself.[6] As shown in Graph 1, beginning in 1786 and continuing to 1810, the *situado* payment never amounted to even 15 percent of the total collected in the Provincias Internas themselves. The *situados* were not the only moneys flowing from Mexico City to the *cajas* of the Provincias Internas. However, the sums listed as coming from Mexico City or Guadalajara cannot be factored into this discussion because they contain,

[5]Velázquez, *La frontera norte*, 7.

[6]The term "total collections" means the amount given as income less the sums recorded for the surplus for the previous year (*existencia*), any amount remitted to the treasury from elsewhere (*otras tesorerías*), amounts reserved in the treasury (*depositos*), amounts held for special purposes (*real hacienda en común*), etc.

hidden in the total amounts, coins that had passed to the capital for reminting and had been returned.[7]

Graphs 2 through 7 demonstrate equally clearly the purposes for which those funds were used. The *cajas* of Arizpe, Chihuahua, and Saltillo outspent the revenues generated in their area in helping to defray the costs of maintaining security there. Some of the expenditures were listed directly as *extraordinario de guerra*, but others were recorded under the rubric of payments (also called *situados*) to other *cajas*. Although Graph 7 demonstrates that overall revenues outpaced expenditures, that happy result came from substantial surpluses generated in the *caja* of Durango and that of Los Alamos, Rosario, and Cosalá.

Nevertheless, the accounts portray an efficient and well-designed system that functioned fairly smoothly, considering distance and other complicating factors. Regrettably, the records are not as revealing as historians might hope for since they often say *otras tesorerías* rather than name any specific one, but they do indicate approximately where the three *cajas* with constant deficits were sending their funds.

In the west, Durango relayed payments to Chihuahua, which forwarded some of the funds to Arizpe. On the eastern side, San Luis Potosí shipped moneys to Saltillo. Once the payments had reached the *cajas*, they were sent out to smaller localities. For example, Arizpe helped support the presidios of Altar, Bacoachí, Bavispe, Buenavista, Fronteras, San Buenaventura, San Carlos, Santa Cruz, and Tucson as well as the towns of Cerrogordo, Parras, and Tubac. Chihuahua handled the central area with payments to presidios in El Principe, San Buenaventura, San Eleazario, and Santa Fe as well as to the towns of Cerrogordo to the south and El Paso del Norte to the north. And Saltillo dispatched its shipments to presidios at Aguaverde, La Bahía, Monclova, and San Antonio as well as to the town of Lampazos.[8] During the decade from 1794 to 1804 alone, Saltillo sent 90 percent or more of its net revenue to other Provincias Internas. The *cajas* were able to do this because for most of the period under discussion they collected considerable surpluses that do not show up in the amounts listed as net income. Some, like Saltillo, collected relatively large amounts from taxes on mining, while

[7]Professor John TePaske, personal communication, June 9, 1991. Equally useless for the same reason are the figures for remissions to those *cajas* from the Provincias Internas.

[8]This network was assembled through the use of the map, "The Presidios of Northern New Spain, 1772–1800," in Max Moorhead, *The Presidio: Bastion of the Spanish Borderlands* (Norman: University of Oklahoma Press, 1975), 62–63. It also contains information from TePaske, personal communication, June 9, 1991, and John Jay TePaske and Herbert S. Klein, *Ingresos y egresos de la Real Hacienda de Nueva España* (Mexico: Instituto Nacional de Antropología e Historia, 1986).

others, without mining, could gather substantial sums from the recently established tobacco monopoly.

This system of payments facilitated the growth of a fiscal and commercial network operating in the north of New Spain, with much of its benefits presumably remaining there. For example, Ramón Gutiérrez points out the development of dependent relations between residents of Santa Fe, New Mexico, and the merchants of Chihuahua, which sound almost exactly like those between government officials and the residents of Oaxaca during the same period.[9] Although Mexico City, Guadalajara, and Guanajuato made substantial contributions to the Provincias Internas and the treasuries there sent coins to mints in the center for restamping, the presidios and towns on the northern frontier maintained connections largely with their disbursing *cajas*, oblivious to their central suppliers farther to the south.

In effect, during the decades since the establishment of the Provincias Internas, the northern region developed into two separate areas: *el norte grande* (the Californias, New Mexico, and Texas) and *el norte chico* (Sonora, Sinaloa, Chihuahua, Durango, and Coahuila), to borrow terms used in Chile. During colonial times, *el norte grande* and its towns and presidios were dependent both economically and militarily on funds, troops, and trade with *el norte chico*, which itself had much stronger ties with central Mexico. Consequently, the two northern areas had come to form an administrative unit somewhat separate from the rest of the viceroyalty but still very dependent upon it. In part, for that reason, the Provincias Internas were unable to take advantage of the proclamation of independence from the Spanish empire in 1821 to break away from Mexico City and dissolve into a separate nation or nations, if indeed they had wanted to.[10]

Yet for political leaders in the center, distance, not revenues, separated them from their counterparts in both *el norte chico* and *el norte grande*, despite fantasies to the contrary. For example, in 1800, as shown in Graph 8, the *cajas* in the Provincias Internas collected substantial revenues without any assistance from elsewhere. In fact, its five *cajas* together, by

---

[9]See Ramón A. Gutiérrez, *When Jesus Came, the Corn Mothers Went Away: Marriage, Sexuality, and Power in New Mexico, 1500–1845* (Stanford: Stanford University Press, 1991), 300–304; and Brian R. Hamnett, *Politics and Trade in Southern Mexico, 1750–1821* (Cambridge, England: Cambridge University Press, 1971), chaps. 1, 3, and 6.

[10]For evidence that various areas did not wish to separate from Mexico see Jaime E. Rodríguez O., "La Constitución de 1824 y la formación del Estado mexicano," *Historia Mexicana* 40, no. 3 (January–March 1991): 517–518 for the Ayuntamiento de Béjar (San Antonio); and Ignacio Almaia Bay, "Polvora, plomo y pinole: Algunas consideraciones generales sobre Sonora alrededor de 1821," in *Simposio de Historia y Antropología de Sonora* (Hermosillo: Instituto de Investigaciones Históricas de la Universidad de Sonora, 1989), 1:293–300 for Sonora.

themselves, gathered the third largest revenues on the Mexican mainland, coming after the giants of Mexico City and Veracruz and surpassing both the individual treasuries of Guadalajara and Guanajuato.[11] Nevertheless, the perception persisted among those who mattered at Chilpancingo and elsewhere that the Provincias Internas were a burden on the treasury.

Based on what historians now know about how viceregal obligations, wars of independence, and damage to mining accelerated the fiscal disintegration of the Viceroyalty of New Spain and its growing regional-ization, it is easy to assume that the process of integration among the Provincias Internas, separate and apart from the center, speeded up and deepened as well. Although for the sake of consistency Graphs 2 through 7 only depict the period from 1780 to 1810, complete records cease after 1813, making it impossible to pinpoint the exact unraveling of the system so carefully elaborated from 1769 onward. Doubtless it suffered the same fate that plagued the rest of the viceroyalty; even by 1813 the accounts depict the imposition of the famous forced loans, the new taxes for war, and the other fiscal signs of extreme crisis.[12] However, scholars can only assume the amount of revenue that was no longer shipped south to Mexico City for reminting or anything else.

The Assumption of Power

When Mexico became independent in 1821, it inherited from Spain the Provincias Internas to the north and the Captaincy General of Guatemala to the south.[13] Although historians have usually accepted that legacy without question, it would not have been out of the realm of possibility for the Provincias Internas to have broken away from Mexico, as did regions of other viceroyalties. As a matter of fact, there is simply no reason for

[11]These figures have been completely disaggregated thanks to TePaske's communication of June 9, 1991, which separates those funds going to the larger *cajas* for reminting.

[12]For more on this see John Jay TePaske, "The Financial Disintegration of the Royal Government of Mexico during the Epoch of Independence," in *The Independence of Mexico and the Creation of the New Nation*, ed. Jaime E. Rodríguez O. (Los Angeles: UCLA Latin American Center Publications, 1989), 63–83.

[13]Certainly the Provincias Internas to the north and the Audiencia of Guatemala are not fully comparable. The latter was historically a more independent entity, although still a part of the Viceroyalty of New Spain and physically contiguous to that part of the viceroyalty which became the nation of Mexico with Independence. Nevertheless, it is reasonable to suppose that had the Provincias Internas been allowed to develop with its own administrator as had been planned in 1776, it too would have had a more separate indentity, although probably not as distinct as that of the Audiencia of Guatemala.

scholars to accept unquestioningly the union of the Provincias Internas with the rest of Mexico. Indeed, the precedents would argue strongly for the reverse, as with the Viceroyalty of La Plata, created in the same year as the Provincias Internas. After Independence it split into at least three separate countries: Argentina, Paraguay, and Uruguay.[14] In another case, that of Chile, which had been made a captaincy general in 1778 under the jurisdiction of the Viceroyalty of Peru—a situation completely equivalent to that of Guatemala and somewhat analogous to that of the Provincias Internas—it too became a separate nation when given the opportunity to become independent from Spain.

In the face of such compelling examples (and in light of the disintegration in 1991 of the Soviet Union and the separation of major components of the former Russian empire), it would seem that historians have been much too accepting of what appears uncritically to have been a fait accompli—that is, the creation of the Mexican nation out of the remains of the Viceroyalty of New Spain. The rest of this essay will be devoted to making some extremely tentative suggestions about the relationship between the former Provincias Internas and the Mexican national government before the war with the United States in 1846.

Political leaders in Mexico City and other centers of power associated with it continued to treat the north ambivalently during most of the rest of the nineteenth century. For example, during the first federal republic, legislators never reached a consensus on how the former Provincias Internas would be incorporated into the Mexican republic. The Constitutional Convention of 1824 decided that New Mexico and the Californias would be considered territories rather than full-fledged states, while it granted that status to Chiapas even though it had been part of the Mexican republic for little more than a year. The present-day states of Sinaloa and Sonora were lumped together fiscally under the rubric of Occidente; Coahuila and Texas were joined together in a makeshift arrangement; and, most disturbing of all, treasury accounts put all the expense figures for Nuevo Léon, Coahuila-Texas, Tamaulipas, and San Luis Potosí under the heading for the latter, as though the other areas were stepchildren.[15]

Revenue sources in the former Provincias Internas changed radically after Independence. Whereas those areas had derived their revenues in colonial times principally from mining and the monopoly on tobacco, after 1821 they enriched national coffers with duties levied on the goods that legally entered their newly opened ports and internal customs stations (Graphs 10

[14]Since the dividing line between the Viceroyalty of Peru and the Viceroyalty of La Plata passed through present-day Bolivia, this essay will leave Bolivia aside in terms of which viceroyalty it left.

[15]O'Gorman, *Historia de las divisiones*, 65–74; *Memoria de Hacienda*, for the years 1824–1834.

and 11). For example, Treasury Minister José Ignacio Esteva described the new customshouse established in Mazatlán in 1824: "There was one Custom House officer at this port and he was blind. In January 1825, the Port was composed of two huts of mud and four of straw; now (1827) a Commissary's Office has been established here and the number of houses exceeds 200."[16] He had good reason to be thrilled; the tariffs collected in Mazatlán in just that year totaled $289,926.[17]

Nevertheless, despite the high amounts flowing in from the customshouses in the former Provincias Internas, treasury administrators never managed to achieve any sort of consistent record keeping with regard to the northern states and territories during all of the years of the first federal period. The gunpowder factory in Santa Fe, New Mexico, would appear in reports in one year only to vanish for the next five. The treasury of the state of San Luis Potosí would be responsible for several other states and territories only for expenses, and then never with any predictability. In some years the Californias would be registered separately while in others they were lumped in with other areas or disappeared altogether, despite the fact that the port of Monterey was thriving.

These inconsistencies reflect several important trends growing steadily more apparent as the years went on. First, Mexico City was having great difficulty in maintaining regular personnel and enforcing policy in its northern regional treasuries, or *comisarías*. This problem is understandable in a new republic whose officials were used to a different system or were new to their tasks. These glitches were easily overcome in the beginning by the influx of revenue derived from the foreign loans of 1824 and 1825 and from the development of a steady and profitable trade at the northern ports.

The increases in trade both at the ports and at customs stations inland also reflected important geopolitical shifts. Although the threats from the English, French, and even the Russians in California had gradually subsided, citizens of the United States began to find profitable markets in the Provincias Internas. Some, such as Zebulon Pike, had launched a movement from St. Louis, Missouri, down to Santa Fe as early as 1806–1807, supposedly inaugurating the Santa Fe Trail, which became well traveled in the 1820s and 1830s. Although Mexican authorities put up token resistance, the new traders offered such a welcome source of needed goods that they often left Mexican territories with huge profits, attracting similar merchants there as well. In other areas, the threats were even more overt, as when the Mexican government permitted immigrants from the United States to settle in Texas, a miscalculation that soon led to their arrival in overwhelming

---

[16]*British and Foreign State Papers* (London, 1846), XIV, 865, as quoted by John E. Baur, "The Evolution of a Mexican Trade Policy, 1821–1828," *The Americas* 19 (1963): 234.

[17]*Memoria de Hacienda*, 1828, charts 4–6.

numbers. Rather than putting up strong resistance to outsiders as the Spanish had done, the Mexican government either turned a blind eye or encouraged encroachment in the name of colonization. These shifts unraveled the bonds that had been so carefully tied since the 1760s between *el norte grande* and *el norte chico*.[18]

Other events exacerbated an already dangerous situation. At the same time that traders from the United States appeared, the fortunes of central Mexico, both literally and figuratively, went into a sharp decline. In 1825 a financial crisis in Britain provoked a serious economic collapse in Europe, and trade with Mexico slumped dramatically. As a result of this and other factors the Mexicans defaulted on their loan payments in August 1827.[19] Although the northern ports seemed little affected by the crisis, revenues from Veracruz dropped substantially. That port would suffer yet another disaster with the Spanish invasion of 1829. Consequently, national expenditures earmarked specifically for the former Provincias Internas fell in 1828–1829 by 1.5 million pesos.[20]

The treasury reports for that year and the next are the last that include detailed analyses of how the national government spent its funds. They also are the last that contain lists of payments due, which mostly consist of amounts owed to troops waiting for their salaries. After the installation of the Bustamante-Alamán government in December 1829, the treasury reports for 1830–1831 and 1831–1832 would present no such embarrassing reminders of fiscal insolvency. In fact, the amount spent for the Provincias Internas in 1829–1830 seems quite in keeping with the years before the 1828–1829 disaster—$2,155,404 (1830) versus $2,134,387 (1828)—but that was no doubt due to the Bustamante administration's hefty internal borrowing in the first six months of 1830.[21]

When in 1833 the anticlerical government of Vice President Valentín Gómez Farías tried to fill the national treasury by forcing the Church to divest itself of all nonessential property and taxing its sale, revolts broke out throughout Mexico. Santa Fe pronounced in favor of centralism in the hope that a new governmental system would bring new revenue with which

[18]The best book on this subject is still David J. Weber, *The Mexican Frontier, 1821–1846: The American Southwest under Mexico* (Albuquerque: University of New Mexico Press, 1982).

[19]For more on this see Jaime E. Rodríguez O., *The Emergence of Spanish America: Vicente Rocafuerte and Spanish Americanism, 1808–1832* (Berkeley: University of California Press, 1975), 120–124; and Carlos Marichal, *A Century of Debt Crises in Latin America: From Independence to the Great Depression, 1820–1930* (Princeton: Princeton University Press, 1989), chap. 2.

[20]See *Memoria de Hacienda*, 1827–1828, 1828–1829, 1829–1830.

[21]For more on this see Barbara A. Tenenbaum, *The Politics of Penury: Debts and Taxes in Mexico, 1821–1856* (Albuquerque: University of New Mexico Press, 1986), 33.

to fight against Indian raids and help the treasury.[22] But once the centralist system was in place, Texas took advantage of the opportunity and successfully rebelled against the administration of Antonio López de Santa Anna.

Following the defeat in Texas, the Mexican government under President Anastasio Bustamante reorganized the national treasury system. Rather than creating a greater centralization of disbursements, it decentralized the structure instead.[23] Although the Constitution of 1836 (Las Siete Leyes) eliminated the *contingente*, or state contribution to the national government, under the new system the former states, now called departments, were ordered to use half their revenues to pay for army units either stationed within their borders or in other areas. The 1837–1838 records for departmental disbursements for Sonora and Sinaloa showed how little had changed since colonial times. According to the report for Sonora, which provides sufficient detail only from July 1, 1837, to June 30, 1838, that department paid subsidies to presidial troops at Altar, Bavispe, Bacoachí, Buenavista, Pitic, Santa Cruz, Tubac, and Tucson among others. Sinaloa, for its part, made contributions to presidial troops in Altar, Culiacán, Monterey, Rosario, and San Diego.[24] Although treasury reports are extremely vague on the matter, it would appear as though these two frontier departments and the Provincias Internas in general could expect very little help from the national treasury in Mexico City during the centralist years. At first, pressing financial difficulties in the capital were exacerbated by the French invasion of Veracruz; however, although during the years from 1838 to 1846 the national treasury reported substantially higher revenue collections, expenses too had increased substantially.[25]

The Unmaking of a Fait Accompli

Although, as Graph 9 shows, by 1844 the former Provincias Internas, as a unit, was the third largest producer of revenues for the national treasury, the relationship between the national government and both *el norte chico*

[22]For more on this see Martín González de la Vara, "La política del federalismo en Nuevo México, 1821–1836," *Historia Mexicana* 36, no. 1 (July–September 1986): 49–80.

[23]For more on this see Barbara A. Tenenbaum, "The Chicken and Egg in Mexican History: The Army and State Finances, 1821–1845," in *Five Centuries of Mexican History/México en el medio milenio*, 2 vols., ed. Virginia Guedea and Jaime E. Rodríguez O. (Mexico and Irvine: Instituto de Investigaciones Dr. José María Luis Mora and University of California, Irvine, 1992), 1:355–370.

[24]Archivo General de la Nación, Mexico, Tribunal de Cuentas, vol. 74, ff. 202–205, 206–211, 213.

[25]See Tenenbaum, *The Politics of Penury*, chap. 2.

and *el norte grande* had deteriorated greatly since 1800. The bonds—economic, financial, and military—that had held the two northern regions to the center had frayed almost to the breaking point. However, unlike the situation in 1821 when *el norte chico* and *el norte grande* felt loyal to Mexico and besides were too weak to survive on their own, by 1846 the powerful expansion of the United States presented those living on the frontier with what might have seemed a reasonable alternative. Texas, already overwhelmingly populated by U.S. citizens, led the way: it tried existing as an independent republic. That solution lasted only a short while, until the immigrant majority succeeded in having its country become part of the United States. The Texas example, although it was clearly different from that of New Mexico or California, nevertheless threatened the status quo in those peripheral areas as well.

Given both its history since 1776 and its location, the Provincias Internas developed very differently from the rest of the Mexican nation. Even though that administrative unit was not separate from central Mexico juridically, its economic, military, and political ties made it part of a whole whose connections with the capital after 1821 were often sporadic. The ties that remained, particularly economic, were more often to *el norte chico* than to central Mexico. Therefore, in a very real sense, the encroachment of the United States in *el norte grande* threatened not the Mexican republic at large but *el norte chico*. In effect, thanks to the weakness in the center leading to Mexico's defeat in the war with the United States, Chihuahua lost New Mexico. Following the 1846 war, *el norte chico* suffered a period of readjustment. Trade links with the territory now belonging to the United States continued, but in the absence of official governmental ties they were subject to increased pressure. Merchants from towns near the new border (itself yet to be firmly established) paid gunmen to stir up trouble in Mexico by revolting in favor of a free-trade zone in the area.[26]

The Apaches stepped up their raids into Mexico, although the United States under the terms of the Treaty of Guadalupe Hidalgo (1848) was supposed to keep marauding Indians on its side of the border. Instead, local citizens and fort commanders in the United States made deals with the Indians permitting them free rein in Mexico in exchange for peace in the northern republic. The government of José Joaquín de Herrera established military colonies to take care of the situation, and by 1849 one thousand soldiers complete with staff appeared in Tamaulipas and Coahuila, Chihuahua, and Sonora and Baja California. Although by 1851 one-half of the planned colonies were in place and others were in the process of forming, large areas still lay exposed and defenseless.

[26]R. H. Mason, *Pictures of Life in Mexico* (London: Smith, Elder, and Company, 1851), 218; *El Siglo XIX*, October 28, 1851.

However, the threat from the United States and foreign filibusterers still remained. Many people left Sonora, some seeking gold in California, some just seeking safety elsewhere. Those who stayed, convinced that, as their chronicler Stuart Voss laments, "Mexico City did not truly seem to care," must have believed the article in the *New York Herald* which they read reprinted in *La Voz del Pueblo*, the official state newspaper. It said that "an agent of the Mexican government" had confided that politicians in Mexico City were considering selling Sonora, Chihuahua, and Baja California in order to get money for the treasury and because they could not protect those areas from Indian raids.[27]

Except for the slice of land sold in La Mesilla (the 1854 Gadsden Purchase), *el norte chico* remained part of Mexico. But it continued to have less of a voice in Mexico City than it believed it deserved. For example, even as Richard Sinkin noted the wide diversity of the thirty-five delegates to the Constitutional Convention of 1857 whose origins can be identified—with the conspicuous exception of Ignacio Zaragoza, who was born in Texas—none of the rest of these notables came from anywhere north of Saltillo, although those areas were, of course, represented.[28] *El norte chico* was finally fully incorporated into the Mexican political structure during the Porfiriato, which created the long-sought free-trade zone. Railroads were built connecting the northern border to the center of Mexico as well as to important terminuses in the United States. New investment fostered growth, particularly in Sonora and Chihuahua, which in turn led to their rebellion in 1910, victory in 1917, and the establishment of the notable "Sonoran dynasty" in the 1920s and 1930s.

Conclusion

This essay has shown that the residents of the Provincias Internas demonstrated substantial loyalty to the nation during the period from 1776 to 1846 by consistently making large payments to the viceregal and republican treasuries and by spending their own funds within the region to defray expenses rightfully belonging to Mexico City. Far from being a drain on the imperial or national coffers, as was generally supposed at the time,

[27]Stuart F. Voss, *On the Periphery of Nineteenth-Century Mexico: Sonora and Sinaloa, 1810–1877* (Tucson: University of Arizona Press, 1982), 109–116.
[28]Richard N. Sinkin, *The Mexican Reforma, 1855–1876: A Study of Liberal Nation-Building* (Austin: Institute of Latin American Studies, University of Texas, 1979), 37–38. It is possible that Sinkin was unable to discover biographical information about the delegates from the north.

the figures show that the *norteños* actually provided more succor than their counterparts in most other areas.

These conclusions give rise to a host of new questions for historians to investigate. Scholars on both sides of the border need to look at the relationship between Mexico City and the Provincias Internas not as a fait accompli but as one in which the north chose to participate. Disagreement and even hostility with Mexico City or the national government did not mean that *norteños* lacked a sense of patriotism or of nationality. It is now time for a thorough examination of how such loyalty evolved. Until then, any discussion of the full development of the Mexican political system from the Bourbon reforms until the present will remain incomplete.

Graph 1

Situado Payments vs. Revenues
1780–1810

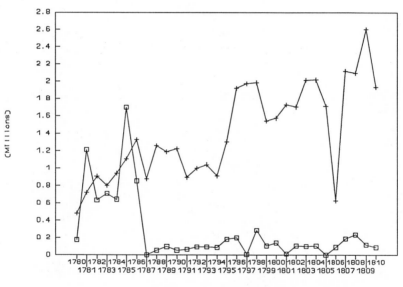

Source: TePaske and Klein, *Ingresos y egresos de la Real Hacienda de Nueva España*, 2:158–210 and passim

Graph 2

Revenues vs. Military Costs
Los Alamos, Rosario, Cosalá, 1780–1810

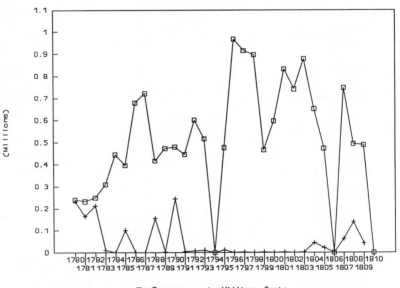

Source: TePaske and Klein, *Ingresos y egresos de la Real Hacienda de Nueva España*, 2:5–27

Graph 3

Revenues vs. Military Costs
Arizpe, 1781–1809

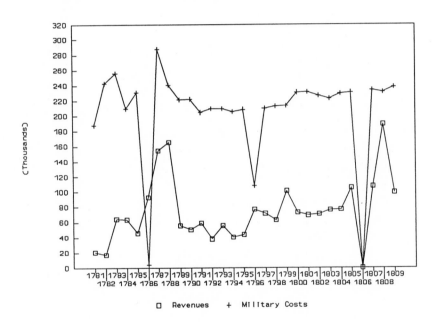

Source: TePaske and Klein, *Ingresos y egresos de la Real Hacienda de Nueva España*, 1:1–15

Graph 4

Revenues vs. Military Costs
Chihuahua, 1785–1790, 1797–1810

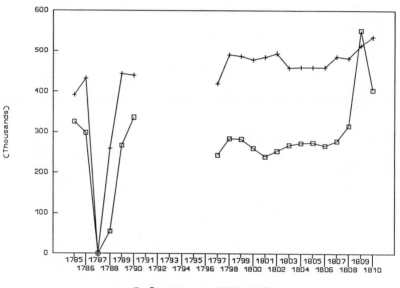

Source: TePaske and Klein, *Ingresos y egresos de la Real Hacienda de Nueva España*, 1:1–15

Graph 5

Revenues vs. Military Costs
Durango, 1780–1810

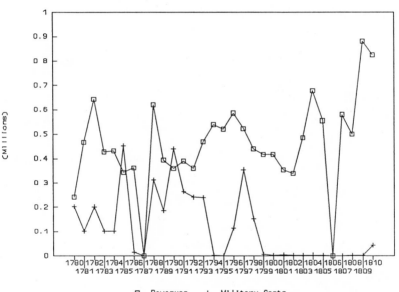

Source: TePaske and Klein, *Ingresos y egresos de la Real Hacienda de Nueva
España*, 1:51–74

Graph 6

Revenues vs. Military Costs
Saltillo, 1794–1810

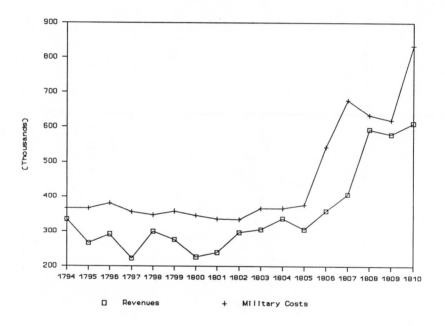

Source: TePaske and Klein, *Ingresos y egresos de la Real Hacienda de Nueva España*, 2:1–10

Graph 7

Revenues vs. Military Costs
Provincias Internas, 1780–1810

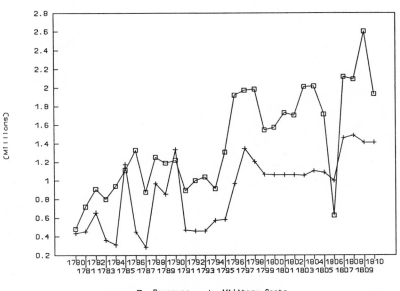

Source: TePaske and Klein, *Ingresos y egresos de la Real Hacienda de Nueva España*, vols. 1 & 2

Graph 8

Revenues in New Spain, 1800

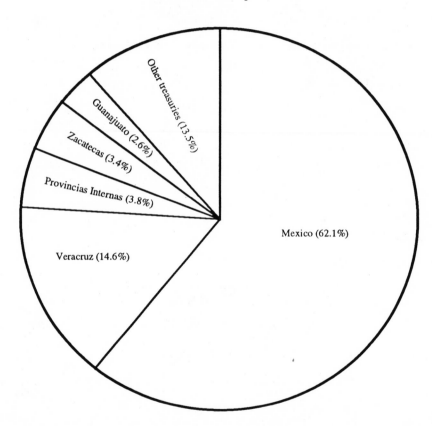

Source: TePaske and Klein, *Ingresos y egresos de la Real Hacienda de Nueva España*, vols. 1 & 2

Graph 9

Revenues in Mexico, 1844

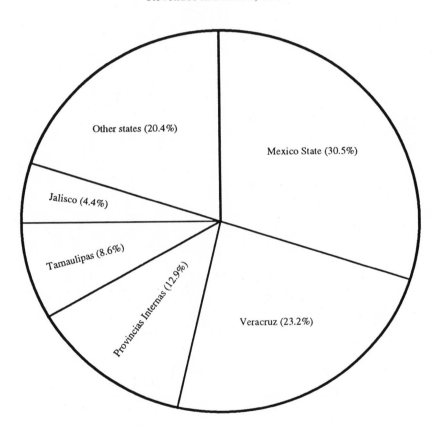

Source: *Memoria de Hacienda*, 1845

Graph 10

Revenues to National Treasury from
Former Provincias Internas, 1825–1834

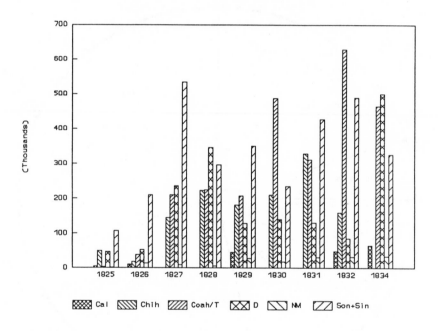

Source: *Memoria de Hacienda*, 1825, 1826, 1827, 1828, 1829, 1830, 1831,
1832, 1834

Graph 11

Revenues to National Treasury from
Former Provincias Internas, 1836–1844

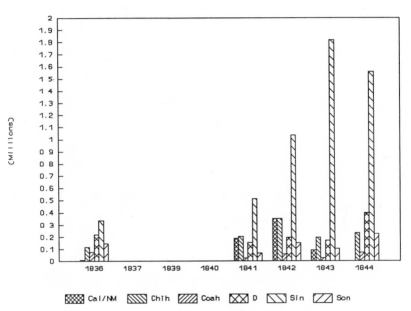

Source: *Memoria de Hacienda*, 1838, 1842, 1843, 1844, 1845

Bibliography

Archives and Special Collections

Archivo General de Indias, Seville
   Sección de México
Archivo General de la Nación, Mexico City
   Ayuntamientos
   Gobernación
   Historia
   Infidencias
   Operaciones de Guerra
   Tribunal de Cuentas
Tulane University Library, New Orleans
   Beruete, Miguel, "Diario de México," 1822–1825

Periodicals

Aguila Mexicana, 1823
El Iris de Jalisco, 1824
Memoria de Hacienda, 1824–1834, 1838, 1842–1845
El Siglo XIX, 1851

Secondary Sources

Adams, John. *The Works of John Adams*. 10 vols. Boston: Little, Brown and Company, 1850–1856.
Alamán, Lucas. *Historia de Méjico desde los primeros movimientos que prepararon su independencia en el año de 1808 hasta la época presente.* 5 vols. Mexico: Imprenta de J. M. Lara, 1849–1852.
———. *Historia de México desde los primeros movimientos que prepararon su independencia en el año de 1808 hasta la época presente.* 5 vols. Mexico: Fondo de Cultura Económica, 1985.

Alba, Antonio de. *Chapala.* Guadalajara: Publicaciones del Banco Industrial de Jalisco, 1954.

Alba, Rafael, ed. *La Constitución de 1812 en la Nueva España.* 2 vols. Mexico: Secretaría de Relaciones Exteriores, Imprenta Guerrero Hnos., 1912–1913.

Almaia Bay, Ignacio. "Polvora, plomo y pinole: Algunas consideraciones generales sobre Sonora alrededor de 1821." In *Simposio de Historia y Antropología de Sonora,* 274–304. Hermosillo: Instituto de Investigaciones Históricas de la Universidad de Sonora, 1989.

Anna, Timothy E. *The Mexican Empire of Iturbide.* Lincoln: University of Nebraska Press, 1990.

Annino, Antonio. "Pratiche creole e liberalismo nella crisi dell spazio urbano coloniale: Il 29 noviembre 1812 a Città del Messico." *Quaderni Storici* (69) 23, no. 3 (December 1988): 727–763.

Archer, Christon I. *The Army in Bourbon Mexico, 1760–1810.* Albuquerque: University of New Mexico Press, 1977.

———. " 'La Causa Buena': The Counterinsurgency Army of New Spain and the Ten Years' War." In *The Independence of Mexico and the Creation of the New Nation,* edited by Jaime E. Rodríguez O., 85–108. Los Angeles: UCLA Latin American Center Publications, 1989.

———. "Where Did All the Royalists Go? New Light on the Military Collapse of New Spain, 1810–1822." In *The Mexican and the Mexican-American Experience in the 19th Century,* edited by Jaime E. Rodríguez O., 24–43. Tempe, AZ: Bilingual Press, 1989.

Barragán y Barragán, José. *Introducción al federalismo.* Mexico: Universidad Nacional Autónoma de México, 1978.

Baur, John E. "The Evolution of a Mexican Trade Policy, 1821–1828." *The Americas* 19 (1963): 225–261.

Benson, Nettie Lee. "The Contested Mexican Election of 1812." *Hispanic American Historical Review* 26 (August 1946): 336–350.

———. *La Diputación Provincial y el federalismo mexicano.* Mexico: El Colegio de México, 1955.

———. "Iturbide y los planes de independencia." *Historia Mexicana* 2, no. 3 (January–March 1953): 439–446.

———. "Servando Teresa de Mier, Federalist." *Hispanic American Historical Review* 28, no. 4 (November 1948): 514–525.

———. "Spain's Contribution to Federalism in Mexico." In *Essays in Mexican History,* edited by Thomas E. Cotner and Carlos Castañeda, 90–103. Austin: Institute of Latin American Studies, University of Texas, 1958.

———. "Texas's Failure to Send a Deputy to the Spanish Cortes, 1810–1812." *Southwestern Historical Quarterly* 64 (July 1960): 1–22.

Benson, Nettie Lee, ed. *Mexico and the Spanish Cortes, 1810–1822.* Austin: University of Texas Press, 1966.

Berry, Charles R. "The Election of Mexican Deputies to the Spanish Cortes, 1810–1822." In *Mexico and the Spanish Cortes, 1810–1822,* edited by Nettie Lee Benson, 10–42. Austin: University of Texas Press, 1966.

Bocanegra, José María. *Memorias para la historia de México independiente, 1822–1846.* 3 vols. Mexico: Fondo de Cultura Económica, 1987.

Brading, David. *Haciendas and Ranchos in the Mexican Bajío: León, 1700–1860.* Cambridge, England: Cambridge University Press, 1978.

———. *Miners and Merchants in Bourbon Mexico.* Cambridge, England: Cambridge University Press, 1971.

Bustamante, Carlos María de. *Diario histórico de México.* 3 vols. Mexico: Instituto Nacional de Antropología, 1980–1984.

———. *Martirologio de algunos de los primeros insurgentes por la libertad e independencia de la América mexicana.* Mexico: Impreso por J. M. Lara, 1841.

Cárdenas de la Peña, Enrique. *Historia marítima de México: Guerra de independencia, 1810–1821.* Mexico: Ediciones Olimpia, 1973.

Castillo Negrete, Emilio del. *México en el siglo XIX, o sea su historia desde 1800 hasta la época presente.* 19 vols. Mexico: Imprenta del "Universal," 1881.

Castro Gutiérrez, Felipe. *Movimientos populares en Nueva España: Michoacán, 1766–1767.* Mexico: Universidad Nacional Autónoma de México, 1990.

Castro Morales, Efraín. *El federalismo en Puebla.* Puebla: Gobierno del Estado de Puebla, 1987.

Cooper, Donald B. *Epidemic Disease in Mexico City, 1761–1813.* Austin: University of Texas Press, 1965.

Cosío Villegas, Daniel. *La Constitución de 1857 y sus críticos.* Mexico: Secretaría de Educación Pública, 1973.

Cosío Villegas, Daniel, ed. *Historia moderna de México.* 10 vols. Mexico: Editorial Hermes, 1955–1972.

Costeloe, Michael P. "Generals versus Politicians: Santa Anna and the 1842 Congressional Elections in Mexico." *Bulletin of Latin American Research* 8, no. 2 (1980): 257–274.

———. *La Primera República Federal de México, 1824–1835.* Mexico: Fondo de Cultura Económica, 1975.

Cunniff, Roger L. "Mexican Municipal Reform, 1810–1822." In *Mexico and the Spanish Cortes, 1810–1822*, edited by Nettie Lee Benson, 59–86. Austin: University of Texas Press, 1966.

D. J. C. *Catecismo político arreglado a la Constitución de la Monarquía Española; para la ilustración del Pueblo, instrucción de la juventud, y uso de las escuelas de primeras letras.* Puebla: Imprenta San Felipe Neri, 1820.

Dublán, Manuel, and José María Lozano. *Legislación mexicana.* 34 vols. Mexico: Dublán y Lozano Hijos, 1876–1904.

Falcón, Romana. "Jefes políticos y rebeliones campesinas: Uso y abuso del poder en el Estado de México." In *Patterns of Contention in Mexican History*, edited by Jaime E. Rodríguez O., 243–273. Wilmington, DE: Scholarly Resources, 1992.

Flores Caballero, Romeo. *La contrarrevolución en la independencia: Los españoles en la vida política, social y económica de México, 1804–1838*. Mexico: El Colegio de México, 1969.

Florescano, Enrique. *Origen y desarrollo de los problemas agrarios en México, 1500–1821*. Mexico: Editorial Era, 1976.

———. *Precios del maíz y crisis agrícolas en México, 1708–1810*. Mexico: El Colegio de México, 1969.

Garcíadiego Dantán, Javier. "Revisionistas al paredón." In *Memorias del Simposio de Historiografía Mexicanista*, 219–221. Mexico: Comité Mexicano de Ciencias Históricas, 1990.

Gerhard, Peter. *The North Frontier of New Spain*. Princeton: Princeton University Press, 1982.

Gómez Pedraza, Manuel. *Manifiesto que . . . ciudadano de la República de Méjico dedica a sus compatriotas, o sea una reseña de su vida pública*. 2d ed. Guadalajara: Oficina de Brambillas, 1831.

González de la Vara, Martín. "La política del federalismo en Nuevo México, 1821–1836." *Historia Mexicana* 36, no. 1 (July–September 1986): 49–80.

Guedea, Virginia. "Alzamientos y motines." In *Historia de México*, edited by Miguel León-Portilla, 5:35–50. Mexico: Editorial Salvat, 1974.

———. *En busca de un gobierno alterno: Los Guadalupes de México*. Mexico: Universidad Nacional Autónoma de México, 1992.

———. "The Conspiracies of 1811: Or How the Criollos Learned to Organize in Secret." Paper presented at the conference on the Mexican Wars of Independence, the Empire, and the Early Republic, University of Calgary, April 4–5, 1991.

———. "Criollos y peninsulares en 1808: Dos puntos de vista sobre lo español." Licenciatura thesis, Universidad Iberoamericana, 1964.

———. "De la fidelidad a la infidencia: Los gobernadores de la parcialidad de San Juan." In *Patterns of Contention in Mexican History*, edited by Jaime E. Rodríguez O., 95–123. Wilmington, DE: Scholarly Resources, 1992.

———. "El golpe de Estado de 1808." *Universidad de México: Revista de la Universidad Nacional Autónoma de México* 488 (September 1991): 21–24.

———. *José María Morelos y Pavón: Cronología*. Mexico: Universidad Nacional Autónoma de México, 1981.

———. "Las primeras elecciones populares en la ciudad de México, 1812–1813." *Mexican Studies/Estudios Mexicanos* 7, no. 1 (Winter 1991): 1–28.

———. "Los procesos electorales insurgentes." *Estudios de historia novohispana* 11 (1991): 201–249.

———. "El pueblo de México y las elecciones de 1812." In *La ciudad de México en la primera mitad del siglo XIX*, 2 vols., edited by Regina Hernández Franyuti, 2:125–165. Mexico: Instituto de Investigaciones Dr. José María Luis Mora, 1994.

———. "Secret Societies during New Spain's Independence Movement." Paper presented at the symposium on New Interpretations of Mexican Independence, University of California, Berkeley, April 24, 1989.

———. "En torno a la Independencia y la Revolución." In *The Revolutionary Process in Mexico: Essays on Political and Social Change, 1880–1940*, edited by Jaime E. Rodríguez O., 267–273. Los Angeles: UCLA Latin American Center Publications, 1990.

Guerra, François-Xavier. *Le Mexique: De l'Ancien Régime à la Révolution.* 2 vols. Paris: L'Harmattan, 1985.

Gutiérrez, Ramón A. *When Jesus Came, the Corn Mothers Went Away: Marriage, Sexuality, and Power in New Mexico, 1500–1845.* Stanford: Stanford University Press, 1991.

Hamill, Hugh M., Jr., *The Hidalgo Revolt: Prelude to Mexican Independence.* Gainesville: University of Florida Press, 1960.

———. "Royalist Counterinsurgency in the Mexican War for Independence: The Lessons of 1811." *Hispanic American Historical Review* 53, no. 3 (August 1973): 470–489.

Hamnett, Brian R. *Politics and Trade in Southern Mexico, 1750–1821.* Cambridge, England: Cambridge University Press, 1971.

———. *Roots of Insurgency: Mexican Regions, 1750–1824.* Cambridge, England: Cambridge University Press, 1986.

———. "Royalist Counterinsurgency and the Continuity of Rebellion: Guanajuato and Michoacán, 1813–1820." *Hispanic American Historical Review* 62, no. 1 (February 1982): 19–48.

Hernández Chávez, Alicia. "Comentario." In *Memorias del Simposio de Historiografía Mexicanista*, 211–213. Mexico: Comité Mexicano de Ciencias Históricas, 1990.

———. "La Guardia Nacional y movilización política de los pueblos." In *Patterns of Contention in Mexican History*, edited by Jaime E. Rodríguez O., 207–225. Wilmington, DE: Scholarly Resources, 1992.

Hernández y Dávalos, Juan E. *Colección de documentos para la historia de la guerra de independencia de México de 1808 a 1821.* 6 vols. Mexico: Biblioteca de "El Sistema Postal de la República Mexicana," José María Sandoval, 1877–1882.

Herrejón Peredo, Carlos, ed. *Actas de la Diputación Provincial de Nueva España, 1820–1821.* Mexico: Cámara de Diputados, 1985.

Iturbide, Agustín de. "Plan de la Independencia de la América Septentrional." In *1810–1821: Documentos básicos para la independencia*, edited by Rene Cárdenas Barrios, 274–286. Mexico: Ediciones del Sector Eléctrico, 1979.

Katz, Friedrich, ed. *Riot, Rebellion, and Revolution: Rural Social Conflict in Mexico.* Princeton: Princeton University Press, 1988.

King, James F. "The Colored Castes and the American Representation in the Cortes of Cádiz." *Hispanic American Historical Review* 33 (February 1953): 33–64.

Knight, Alan. "Interpretaciones recientes de la Revolución Mexicana." In *Memorias del Simposio de Historiografía Mexicanista*, 193–205. Mexico: Comité Mexicano de Ciencias Históricas, 1990.

————. *The Mexican Revolution*. 2 vols. Cambridge, England: Cambridge University Press, 1988.

Ladd, Doris. *The Mexican Nobility at Independence, 1780–1826*. Austin: Institute of Latin American Studies, University of Texas, 1976.

Lira, Andrés. *Comunidades indígenas frente a la ciudad de México: Tenochtitlan y Tlatelolco, sus pueblos y barrios, 1812–1919*. Zamora: El Colegio de Michoacán, 1983.

Macune, Charles. *El Estado de México y la federación mexicana*. Mexico: Fondo de Cultura Económica, 1978.

Marichal, Carlos. *A Century of Debt Crises in Latin America: From Independence to the Great Depression, 1820–1930*. Princeton: Princeton University Press, 1989.

Mason, R. H. *Pictures of Life in Mexico*. London: Smith, Elder, and Company, 1851.

Mejía Fernández, Miguel. *Política agraria en México en el siglo XIX*. Mexico: Siglo XXI, 1979.

Mexico. *Diario de las sesiones de la Soberana Junta Provisional Gubernativa del Imperio Mexicano*. Mexico: Imprenta Imperial de Alejandro Valdés, 1821.

Mexico, Cámara de Diputados. *Crónicas del Acta Constitutiva*. Mexico: Cámara de Diputados, 1974.

————, ibid. *Crónicas de la Constitución Federal de 1824*. 2 vols. Mexico: Cámara de Diputados, 1974.

————, ibid. *Historia parlamentaria: Sesiones secretas*. 2 vols. Mexico: Instituto de Investigaciones Legislativas, Cámara de Diputados, 1982.

Mexico, Congress. *Actas del Congreso Constituyente Mexicano*. 3 vols. Mexico: Imprenta de Alejandro Valdés, 1823.

————, ibid. *Diario de las sesiones del Congreso constituyente*. 4 vols. Mexico: Oficina de Valdés, 1823.

Michelena, José Mariano. "Verdadero origen de la revolución de 1809 en el Departamento de Michoacán." In *Documentos históricos mexicanos*, 7 vols., edited by Genaro García. 2d ed. Mexico: Secretaría de Educación Pública, 1985.

Mier, Servando Teresa de. "Memoria político-instructiva enviada desde Filadelfia en agosto de 1821 a los gefes independientes del Anáhuac, llamado por los españoles Nueva España." In *La formación de un republicano*, vol. 4 of *Obras Completas*, edited by Jaime E. Rodríguez O., 164. Mexico: Universidad Nacional Autónoma de México, 1988.

Mirafuentes, José Luis. *Movimientos de resistencia y rebeliones indígenas en el norte de México*. Mexico: Universidad Nacional Autónoma de México, 1989.

Miranda, José. *Las ideas y las instituciones políticas mexicanas: Primera parte, 1521–1820*. 2d ed. Mexico: Instituto de Investigaciones Jurídicas, Universidad Nacional Autónoma de México, 1978.

Moorhead, Max. *The Presidio: Bastion of the Spanish Borderlands*. Norman: University of Oklahoma Press, 1975.

Morin, Claude. *Michoacán en la Nueva España del siglo XVIII*. Mexico: Fondo de Cultura Económica, 1979.

Nava Oteo, Guadalupe. *Cabildos de la Nueva España en 1808*. Mexico: Secretaría de Educación Pública, 1973.

Noriega Elío, Cecilia. *El Constituyente de 1842*. Mexico: Universidad Nacional Autónoma de México, 1986.

Ocampo, Javier. *Las ideas de un día: El pueblo mexicano ante la consumación de su Independencia*. Mexico: El Colegio de México, 1969.

O'Gorman, Edmundo. *Historia de las divisiones territoriales de México*. Mexico: Editorial Porrúa, 1966.

Olagaray, Roberto, ed. *Colección de Documentos Históricos Mexicanos*. 4 vols. Mexico: Antigua Imprenta de Murgía, 1924.

Parcero, María de la Luz. "El liberalismo triunfante y el surgimiento de la historia nacional." In *Investigaciones contemporáneas sobre historia de México: Memorias de la Tercera Reunión de Historiadores Mexicanos y Norteamericanos*, 443–457. Mexico and Austin: Universidad Nacional Autónoma de México, El Colegio de México, and University of Texas, 1971.

Perry, Laurens Ballard. *Juárez and Díaz: Machine Politics in Mexico*. DeKalb: Northern Illinois University Press, 1978.

Puebla. *Acta de la Junta de Puebla sobre la reinstalación del congreso mexicano*. Puebla: Oficina de D. Pedro de la Rosa, 1823.

Reina, Leticia. *Las rebeliones campesinas en México, 1819–1906*. Mexico: Siglo XXI, 1980.

Rodríguez O., Jaime E. "El *Bosquejo ligerísimo de la revolución de Mégico* de Vicente Rocafuerte." Paper prepared for the Seminario de Historiografía de México, Instituto de Investigaciones Históricas, Universidad Nacional Autónoma de México, March 1992.

———. "La Constitución de 1824 y la formación del Estado mexicano." *Historia Mexicana* 40, no. 3 (January–March 1991): 507–535.

———. *Down from Colonialism: Mexico's Nineteenth-Century Crisis*. Los Angeles: Chicano Studies Research Center, University of California, Los Angeles, 1983.

———. *The Emergence of Spanish America: Vicente Rocafuerte and Spanish Americanism, 1808–1832*. Berkeley: University of California Press, 1975.

———. "From Royal Subject to Republican Citizen: The Role of the Autonomists in the Independence of Mexico." In *The Independence of Mexico and the Creation of the New Nation*, edited by Jaime E. Rodríguez O., 19–43. Los Angeles: UCLA Latin American Center Publications, 1989.

———. "La historiografía de la Primera República." In *Memorias del Simposio de Historiografía Mexicanista*, 147–159. Mexico: Comité Mexicano de Ciencias Históricas, 1990.

————. "Intellectuals and the Mexican Constitution of 1824." In *Los intelectuales y el poder en México*, edited by Roderic Ai Camp, Charles Hale, and Josefina Zoraida Vázquez, 63–74. Mexico and Los Angeles: El Colegio de México and UCLA Latin American Center Publications, 1991.

————. "La paradoja de la independencia de México." *Secuencia: Revista de historia y ciencias sociales* 21 (September–December 1991): 7–17.

————. "The Struggle for Dominance: The Legislature versus the Executive in Early Mexico." Paper presented at the conference on The Mexican Wars of Independence, the Empire, and the Early Republic, University of Calgary, April 4–5, 1991.

————. "The Struggle for the Nation: The First Centralist-Federalist Conflict in Mexico." *The Americas* 49, no. 1 (July 1992): 1–22.

————. "Two Revolutions: France 1789 and Mexico 1810." *The Americas* 47, no. 2 (October 1990): 161–176.

Rodríguez O., Jaime E., ed. *Patterns of Contention in Mexican History.* Wilmington, DE: Scholarly Resources, 1992.

Salvucci, Richard J. *Textiles and Capitalism in Mexico: An Economic History of the Obrajes, 1539–1840.* Princeton: Princeton University Press, 1987.

Santoni, Pedro. "A Fear of the People: The Civic Militia of Mexico in 1845." *Hispanic American Historical Review* 68, no. 2 (May 1988): 269–288.

Scholes, Walter V. *Mexican Politics during the Juárez Regime, 1855–1872.* Columbia: University of Missouri Press, 1957.

Sinkin, Richard N. *The Mexican Reforma, 1855–1876: A Study of Liberal Nation-Building.* Austin: Institute of Latin American Studies, University of Texas, 1979.

Super, John. "Querétaro Obrajes: Industry and Society in Provincial Mexico." *Hispanic American Historical Review* 56, no. 2 (May 1976): 197–216.

Tannenbaum, Frank. *The Mexican Agrarian Revolution.* New York: Macmillan Company, 1929.

Taylor, William B. *Drinking, Homicide, and Rebellion in Colonial Mexican Villages.* Stanford: Stanford University Press, 1979.

Tenenbaum, Barbara A. "The Chicken and Egg in Mexican History: The Army and State Finances, 1821–1845." In *Five Centuries of Mexican History/México en el medio milenio*, 2 vols., edited by Virginia Guedea and Jaime E. Rodríguez O., 1:355–370. Mexico and Irvine: Instituto de Investigaciones Dr. José María Luis Mora and University of California, Irvine, 1992.

————. *The Politics of Penury: Debts and Taxes in Mexico, 1821–1856.* Albuquerque: University of New Mexico Press, 1986.

TePaske, John Jay. "The Financial Disintegration of the Royal Government of Mexico during the Epoch of Independence." In *The Independence of Mexico and the Creation of the New Nation*, edited by Jaime E.

Rodríguez O., 63–83. Los Angeles: UCLA Latin American Center Publications, 1989.

TePaske, John Jay, and Herbert S. Klein. *Ingresos y egresos de la Real Hacienda de Nueva España.* 2 vols. Mexico: Instituto Nacional de Antropología e Historia, 1986.

Torre Villar, Ernesto de la, ed. *Los Guadalupes y la Independencia, con una selección de documentos inéditos.* Mexico: Editorial Porrúa, 1985.

Tutino, John. *From Insurrection to Revolution in Mexico: Social Bases of Agrarian Violence, 1750–1940.* Princeton: Princeton University Press, 1986.

Van Young, Eric. *Hacienda and Market in Eighteenth-Century Mexico: The Rural Economy of the Guadalajara Region, 1675–1820.* Berkeley: University of California Press, 1981.

Velázquez, María del Carmen. *La frontera norte y la experiencia colonial.* Archivo Histórico Diplomático Mexicano, cuarta época, num. 11. Mexico: Secretaría de Relaciones Exteriores, 1982.

Villar, Samuel I. del. "Morality and Democracy in Mexico: Some Personal Reflections." In *Sucesión presidencial: The 1988 Mexican Presidential Elections,* edited by Edgar W. Butler and Jorge A. Bustamante, 143–147. Boulder, CO: Westview Press, 1991.

Villaseñor y Villaseñor, Alejandro. *Biografías de los héroes y caudillos de la independencia: Con retratos.* 2 vols. Mexico: Imprenta de "El Tiempo" de Victoriano Argüeros, 1910.

Villegas Moreno, Gloria. "Comentario." In *Memorias del Simposio de Historiografía Mexicanista,* 214–218. Mexico: Comité Mexicano de Ciencias Históricas, 1990.

Villoro, Luis. *El proceso ideológico de la revolución de la independencia.* 2d ed. Mexico: Universidad Nacional Autónoma de México, 1977.

———. *El proceso ideológico de la revolución de la independencia.* 3d ed. Mexico: Universidad Nacional Autónoma de México, 1981.

———. "La revolución de independencia." In *Historia general de México,* 2:303–356. Mexico: El Colegio de México, 1976.

Voss, Stuart F. *On the Periphery of Nineteenth-Century Mexico: Sonora and Sinaloa, 1810–1877.* Tucson: University of Arizona Press, 1982.

Weber, David J. *The Mexican Frontier, 1821–1846: The American Southwest under Mexico.* Albuquerque: University of New Mexico Press, 1982.

Wood, Gordon. *The Radicalism of the American Revolution.* New York: Alfred A. Knopf, 1992.

Zerecero, Anastasio. *Memorias para la historia de las revoluciones en México.* Mexico: Universidad Nacional Autónoma de México, 1976.

Index

Abad y Queipo, Manuel, 16, 41
Acámbaro, 12
Acatlán, 49
Acevedo, Manuel de, 30, 31
Acta constitutiva (1823), 78–79, 83
Adalid, Ignacio, 52
Adams, John, 1
Agriculture, 28, 31, 66
Aguaverde, 89
Aguirre, Guillermo de, 41
Agustín I, 3, 81, 82, 85
Alamán, Lucas, 48, 52, 54, 55, 57, 71, 94
Los Alamos, 88, 89
Alba, José María, 55
Alcalá, José María: as elector, 55–56, 59–61; as Guadalupe, 47–49, 50; proceedings against, 52, 60; votes for, 49
Allende, Ignacio, 50
Alta California, 86, 87, 90, 93
Altar, 89, 95
Alvarez, Melchor, 28–29
América Septentrional, 86
Antigua, 24
Apache Indians, 96
Apodaca, Juan Ruíz de, 25, 26–28, 30, 31, 36
Archer, Christon I.: essay of, 11–37; mentioned, 8
Archivo General de la Nación, 73, 74
Argentina, 92
Argüelles, Miguel, 78
Arias de Villafañe, José, 55
Arizona, 86
Arizpe, 86, 88, 89, 101
Army of the Center, 13

Army of New Spain: defeat of, 36–37; financial obligations of, 31; fiscal crisis of, 31, 34–36; Hidalgo rebellion and, 11; offenses of commanders, 29, 32–34; politicization of, 8, 11–37; power and, 2, 8, 28–30, 34; recruitment, 30
Army of the Right, 12
Army of the South, 19, 28
Army of the Three Guarantees, 37
Arroyave, Francisco de, 49
Ascorve, Manuel, 57, 59, 60
Audiencia, 15, 41, 43, 47, 68
Autonomists and autonomy, 4, 53, 62, 72
Ayuntamiento of Béjar, 75
Ayuntamiento of Mérida, 75
Ayuntamiento of Mexico City, 40, 41, 51–52, 53–54
Ayuntamientos: elections and, 44, 46–54, 56; formation of, 43, 68; goal of, 49; gubernatorial power and, 72; necessity of local governments and, 75; political role of, 40, 43, 68, 70, 74; representation of provinces and, 41, 69; restoration of, 71

Bacoachí, 89, 95
La Bahía, 89
Baja California: control over, 87; government of, 86; independence and, 87; mentioned, 90, 93; population estimates, 87; soldiers in, 96; as territory, 93

Latin American Silhouettes
Studies in History and Culture

William H. Beezley and
Judith Ewell
Editors

Volumes Published

William H. Beezley and Judith Ewell, eds., *The Human Tradition in Latin America: The Twentieth Century* (1987).
Cloth ISBN 0-8420-2283-X
Paper ISBN 0-8420-2284-8

Judith Ewell and William H. Beezley, eds., *The Human Tradition in Latin America: The Nineteenth Century* (1989).
Cloth ISBN 0-8420-2331-3
Paper ISBN 0-8420-2332-1

David G. LaFrance, *The Mexican Revolution in Puebla, 1908–1913: The Maderista Movement and the Failure of Liberal Reform* (1989).
ISBN 0-8420-2293-7

Mark A. Burkholder, *Politics of a Colonial Career: José Baquíjano and the Audiencia of Lima*, 2d ed. (1990).
Cloth ISBN 0-8420-2353-4
Paper ISBN 0-8420-2352-6

Carlos B. Gil, ed., *Hope and Frustration: Interviews with Leaders of Mexico's Political Opposition* (1992).
Cloth ISBN 0-8420-2395-X
Paper ISBN 0-8420-2396-8

Heidi Zogbaum, *B. Traven: A Vision of Mexico* (1992). ISBN 0-8420-2392-5

Jaime E. Rodríguez O., ed., *Patterns of Contention in Mexican History* (1992). ISBN 0-8420-2399-2

Louis A. Pérez, Jr., ed., *Slaves, Sugar, and Colonial Society: Travel Accounts of Cuba, 1801–1899* (1992).
Cloth ISBN 0-8420-2354-2
Paper ISBN 0-8420-2415-8

Peter Blanchard, *Slavery and Abolition in Early Republican Peru* (1992).
Cloth ISBN 0-8420-2400-X
Paper ISBN 0-8420-2429-8

Paul J. Vanderwood, *Disorder and Progress: Bandits, Police, and Mexican Development*. Revised and Enlarged Edition (1992).
Cloth ISBN 0-8420-2438-7
Paper ISBN 0-8420-2439-5

Sandra McGee Deutsch and Ronald H. Dolkart, eds., *The Argentine Right: Its History and Intellectual Origins, 1910 to the Present* (1993).
Cloth ISBN 0-8420-2418-2
Paper ISBN 0-8420-2419-0

Steve Ellner, *Organized Labor in Venezuela, 1958–1991: Behavior and Concerns in a Democratic Setting* (1993). ISBN 0-8420-2443-3

Paul J. Dosal, *Doing Business with the Dictators: A Political History of United Fruit in Guatemala, 1899–1944* (1993). Cloth ISBN 0-8420-2475-1   Paper ISBN 0-8420-2590-1

Marquis James, *Merchant Adventurer: The Story of W. R. Grace* (1993). ISBN 0-8420-2444-1

John Charles Chasteen and Joseph S. Tulchin, eds., *Problems in Modern Latin American History: A Reader* (1994). Cloth ISBN 0-8420-2327-5
Paper ISBN 0-8420-2328-3

Marguerite Guzmán Bouvard, *Revolutionizing Motherhood: The Mothers of the Plaza de Mayo* (1994).
Cloth ISBN 0-8420-2486-7
Paper ISBN 0-8420-2487-5

William H. Beezley, Cheryl English Martin, and William E. French, eds., *Rituals of Rule, Rituals of Resistance: Public Celebrations and Popular Culture in Mexico* (1994). Cloth ISBN 0-8420-2416-6 Paper ISBN 0-8420-2417-4

Stephen R. Niblo, *War, Diplomacy, and Development: The United States and Mexico, 1938–1954* (1995). ISBN 0-8420-2550-2

G. Harvey Summ, ed., *Brazilian Mosaic: Portraits of a Diverse People and Culture* (1995). Cloth ISBN 0-8420-2491-3 Paper ISBN 0-8420-2492-1

N. Patrick Peritore and Ana Karina Galve-Peritore, eds., *Biotechnology in Latin America: Politics, Impacts, and Risks* (1995). Cloth ISBN 0-8420-2556-1 Paper ISBN 0-8420-2557-X

Silvia Marina Arrom and Servando Ortoll, eds., *Riots in the Cities: Popular Politics and the Urban Poor in Latin America, 1765–1910* (1996). Cloth ISBN 0-8420-2580-4 Paper ISBN 0-8420-2581-2

Roderic Ai Camp, ed., *Polling for Democracy: Public Opinion and Political Liberalization in Mexico* (1996). ISBN 0-8420-2583-9

Brian Loveman and Thomas M. Davies, Jr., eds., *The Politics of Antipolitics: The Military in Latin America*, 3d ed., revised and updated (1996). Cloth ISBN 0-8420-2609-6 Paper ISBN 0-8420-2611-8

Joseph S. Tulchin, Andrés Serbín, and Rafael Hernández, eds., *Cuba and the Caribbean: Regional Issues and Trends in the Post-Cold War Era* (1997). ISBN 0-8420-2652-5

Thomas W. Walker, ed., *Nicaragua without Illusions: Regime Transition and Structural Adjustment in the 1990s* (1997). Cloth ISBN 0-8420-2578-2 Paper ISBN 0-8420-2579-0

Dianne Walta Hart, *Undocumented in L.A.: An Immigrant's Story* (1997). Cloth ISBN 0-8420-2648-7 Paper ISBN 0-8420-2649-5

Jaime E. Rodríguez O. and Kathryn Vincent, eds., *Myths, Misdeeds, and Misunderstandings: The Roots of Conflict in U.S.-Mexican Relations* (1997). ISBN 0-8420-2662-2

Jaime E. Rodríguez O. and Kathryn Vincent, eds., *Common Border, Uncommon Paths: Race, Culture, and National Identity in U.S.-Mexican Relations* (1997). ISBN 0-8420-2673-8

William H. Beezley and Judith Ewell, eds., *The Human Tradition in Modern Latin America* (1997). Cloth ISBN 0-8420-2612-6 Paper ISBN 0-8420-2613-4

Donald F. Stevens, ed., *Based on a True Story: Latin American History at the Movies* (1997). ISBN 0-8420-2582-0

Jaime E. Rodríguez O., ed., *The Origins of Mexican National Politics, 1808–1847* (1997). Paper ISBN 0-8420-2723-8

Che Guevara, *Guerrilla Warfare*, with revised and updated introduction and case studies by Brian Loveman and Thomas M. Davies, Jr., 3d ed. (1997). Cloth ISBN 0-8420-2677-0 Paper ISBN 0-8420-2678-9

Adrian A. Bantjes, *As If Jesus Walked on Earth: Cardenismo, Sonora, and the Mexican Revolution* (1998). ISBN 0-8420-2653-3

Henry A. Dietz and Gil Shidlo, eds., *Urban Elections in Democratic Latin America* (1998). Cloth ISBN 0-8420-2627-4 Paper ISBN 0-8420-2628-2

A. Kim Clark, *The Redemptive Work: Railway and Nation in Ecuador, 1895–1930* (1998). ISBN 0-8420-2674-6

Joseph S. Tulchin, ed., with Allison M. Garland, *Argentina: The Challenges of Modernization* (1998). ISBN 0-8420-2721-1